סדר ט״ו בשבט

SEDER TU BISHEVAT

THE FESTIVAL OF TREES

—— ADAM FISHER ——

CCAR
PRESS

CENTRAL CONFERENCE OF AMERICAN RABBIS

Copyright © 1989
Central Conference of American Rabbis
192 Lexington Ave., New York, NY 10016

ISBN: 0-88123-008-1

Printed in the United States of America

LIBRARY OF CONGRESS INFORMATION:

Fisher, Adam. 1941-
    Seder Tu Bishevat: the festival of trees / written and edited by Adam Fisher
        p. 97
    English and romanized Hebrew.
    Title on half t.p. : Seder 15 bi-Shevat = Seder Tu Bishevat.
    ISBN 0-88123-008-1: $6.95
    1. Tu bi-Shevat — Prayer-books and devotions.   2. Judaism — Prayer-books and devotions —
English.   3. Judaism — Prayer-books and devotions — Hebrew.
    I. Title.   II. Title: Seder 15 bi-Shevat.   III. Title: Seder Tu bi-Shevat.
    BM695.T9F57   1989
    296.4'39 — dc20   89 — 25212

CENTRAL CONFERENCE OF AMERICAN RABBIS

The Conference is the professional association of Reform rabbis in the United States, Canada and abroad, founded in 1889 by Isaac Mayer Wise. It is the largest publisher of Jewish liturgy in the world. Other related publications include: *Haneirot Halalu, A Home Celebration of Chanuka (1989); Gates of Mitzvah (1979); Gates of the Seasons* (1983); *Shabbat Manual (1972); Gates of the House (1977); The Five Scrolls (1984)* and *A Passover Haggadah (1974).* Write for a complete catalogue.

ACKNOWLEDGMENTS

I express my deep thanks for the encouragement and help offered by my colleagues Rabbis Herbert Bronstein, H. Leonard Poller, Peter Knobel and Stephen Pearce who chaired the Liturgy, Reform Jewish Practices and Publications Committees. To them and their committees go my deep appreciation.

I am grateful to Rabbi Joseph B. Glaser for his suggestion that I begin this project and for his support throughout.

Rabbi Elliot L. Stevens has my deepest gratitude for his continual encouragement and wise guidance. His editorial expertise, knowledge of music and good judgment were invaluable. I cannot overestimate his contribution to this Seder.

I wish to acknowledge with thanks the many colleagues who shared Tu BiShevat material they have used in their communities. Some of that material is reflected in these pages; all of it was helpful.

I am grateful to Steve Manowitz of Palinurus Productions for his dedication to this book.

My thanks to Deborah Fisher for the graphics.

Rabbis Alan Flam, Philip Bentley and Steven Moss provided valuable advice along the way.

I am grateful to my friend and colleague, Cantor Michael F. Trachtenberg, who was extremely helpful with some of the music.

The Librarians of Hebrew Union College-Jewish Institute of Religion in New York and Cincinnati were most gracious in sending essential material.

My deep appreciation to the people of Temple Isaiah, Stony Brook for encouraging me to take the time to work on this project, for their enthusiasm, extraordinary support and love. May we celebrate many Tu BiShevat sedarim together in health and in joy.

To Eileen, Rachel and Deborah go my love and thanks for their support.

My heartfelt appreciation to David Axelrod, Steve Weitzman and Bob Yarmus, dear friends, who have contributed more to this project than they know.

A.F.

AKNOWLEDGMENTS

Every effort has been made to ascertain the owners of copyrights for the selections used in this volume, and to obtain permission to reprint copyrighted passages. For the use of the passages indicated, the Central Conference of American Rabbis expresses its gratitude to those whose names appear below. The Conference will be pleased, in subsequent editions, to correct any inadvertent errors or omissions that may be pointed out.

BANTAM BOOKS, INC.: From *Seasons of Our Joy* , by Arthur Waskow. Copyright© 1982 and Copyright© 1987 Bantam Books.

"The Tree and the Mashiach" from *Nine Entered Paradise Alive,* by Danny Siegel. Copyright© 1980.

"Tu B'Shevat" in *Especially Wonderful Days,* By Rabbi Steven Carr Reuben.

ACUM LTD.: "Eretz Zavat Chalav," Lyrics: Traditional, Music: Eliahu Gamliel, Copyright© by Edition NEGEN Israel; "Tsadik Katamar", Lyrics: Traditional, Music: Avi Maslo, Copyright© Or-Tav Music Publ.; "Nitzanim Niru", Lyrics: Traditional, Music: Nachum Heiman, Copyright© by Mifalei Tarbut Vechinuch, Israel; "Havu Lanu Yayin", Lyrics: Matatyahu Shelem, Music M. Shelem, Copyright© Mifalei Tarbut Vechinuch, Israel; "El Ginat Egoz", Lyrics: Traditional, Music: Sara Levy-Tanai, Copyright© by the author, Israel; "Hashkediyah" Lyrics: Israel Dushman, Music: Menashe Ravina, Copyright© by the authors, Israel.

HARCOURT BRACE JOVANOVICH, INC.: The poem "Fueled," from *Serve Me a Slice of Moon,* by Marcie Hans, Copyright© 1965, reprinted by permission of Harcourt Brace Jonavich, Inc.

TRANSCONTINENTAL MUSIC PUBLICATIONS: Dr. Judith Tischler, for the use of selections in *Gates of Song,* Copyright© 1987.

TARA PUBLICATIONS: *The Shepardic - Oriental Songbook,* Edited by Velvel Pasternak:"Eits Rimon" by Y. Gorchov, adapted from a Persian melody, Copyright© 1983.

JEWISH NATIONAL FUND: *Tu Bi'Shevat Manual,* Edited by S. Goldman, Copyright© 1984.

CHAPPELL MUSIC LTD.: "Jerusalem of Gold" by Naomi Shemer, Copyright© 1967. All rights reserved. Used by permission.

LIVERIGHT PUBLISHING CORP., INC.: Poem "i thank you God" by E. E. Cummings, from XAIPE, by E.E. Cummungs, ed. by George James Firmage. Copyright© 1979, 1978, 1973 by Nancy T. Andrews. Copyright© 1979, 1973 by George James Firmage.

JEWISH PUBLICATION SOCIETY OF AMERICA: Trasliterations from *Tanakh,* Copyright© 1962, 1967, 1985.

SINGING WIND PRESS: *Gathering the Sparks,* by Howard Schwartz, Copyright© 1979.

"The New Year For Trees" by Howard Schwartz, reprinted from *Gathering the sparks* (St. Louis, 1979), by permission of Howard Schwartz. Copyright© 1979 by Howard Shwartz.

INTRODUCTION

Tu BiShevat, the fifteenth day of the month of Shevat, has a long and varied background.

Jewish literature of the first several centuries of the Common Era tells us that Tu BiShevat was the new year for trees. It was the anniversary for deciding when the trees in Israel were mature enough so that their fruit could be harvested. This date was also the new year for the annual tithe on fruit trees. Tu BiShevat was the date designated because by then the early winter rains were mostly over and the period of budding was just beginning.

By the 16th century the custom of eating fruit and reciting Psalms on Tu BiShevat, was expanded so that it became a celebration of the Kabbalistic "Tree of Life." This tree is a visual representation of the flow of Divine energy into the world.

In modern times there has been a focus on the reforestation of the Land of Israel. Trees have also been a metaphor for Torah.

Tu BiShevat fits into the cycle of holidays as a celebration of renewal. Rosh Hashanah celebrates the creation of the world. Shabbat is a remembrance of God's work of creation. In the prayer book, we praise God as the one who renews the work of creation daily. Tu BiShevat is the celebration of the renewal of trees and all of nature. The theme of renewal is also found in our celebration of the renewal of the Land of Israel, and in the Kabbalistic tradition which celebrates Tu BiShevat as the renewal of the flow of Divine energy.

Other themes have also been woven through this seder: joy and thankfulness for the beauty and fruit of trees which God has created and sustained and renewed, Torah which is our "Tree of Life," our responsibility to care for God's world of which we are the custodians, and our responsibility for sharing the fruits of God's earth.

Tu BiShevat is a festival full of wonder, joy, acknowledgment and thankfulness as we anticipate the renewal of the natural world.

Using these Sedarim

There are two seder services: Seder I is for use when most of the participants are adults or teenagers; Seder II may be used when there are many children present. Seder II has been written so that children in the fourth grade and above should be able to read it. Younger children should be able to understand it and adults will not find it juvenile. Considerable flexibility of use is possible for both Sedarim, so that both can be simplified or expanded depending on the needs of participants.

Our heritage includes an enormous body of beautiful literature which is relevant to Tu BiShevat. Because there is so much rich material, it is not possible to use all of it at one Seder; therefore, optional material is included along with the basic text.

The basic text is printed in larger serif type while optional supplementary passages follow the symbol ⤳ ⤆ and are printed in smaller sans serif type. The leader may use only the basic text or add considerable supplementary material.

The Seder is also designed so that the leader can choose the passages in the basic text they prefer and omit others, even entire sections, without loss of continuity. In this way, one can plan a very brief seder or one lasting an entire evening.

In place of the conventional rubrics 'Reader,' and 'All Reading,' Roman type is used for 'Reader,' and italics for 'All Reading.' The symbol ♪ denotes a song and the page number indicates the page on which the music is found.

Preparing for the Seder

The table should be set in a festive manner.

Four kinds of wine from white to deep red should be available. (One can simply use red and white wine and mix them to get the desired colors.) Some may wish to use red and white grape juice for children.

At least a few selections of the three different classifications of fruit should be available:

> Fruit with shells — nuts, oranges, pomegranates
> Fruit with pits — dates, olives
> Fruit which is entirely edible — figs, raisins.

Bread should be provided for a motzi.

The main course of the meal can be provided by the host or Synagogue, or everyone can contribute something and make it a pot-luck meal. In keeping with the agricultural orientation of Tu BiShevat, some may wish to make this a vegetarian meal.

There should be candles and challah if the seder is observed on Shabbat.
If planting trees in Israel will be mentioned, order material from the Jewish National Fund.

If planting parsley or romaine to be used on Passover, prepare cups with potting soil, and have seeds available.

Conducting the Seder

For small groups, the participants can take turns reading around the table. The leader may suggest which passages should be read.

For large groups, the leader may take the same approach or do the following: the leader should plan ahead of time which passages will be read; there should be someone to lead the songs, another person to be the story teller, and one or two others who will be readers. The leader can then call upon these people to lead parts of the Seder. This would be instead of having the participants taking turns as the reader. In this way, there will be a change of voice, and involve of those other than the leader, yet the smooth flow of the Seder for a large gathering will be maintained.

It is my hope that this Seder will make your Tu BiShevat a joyous experience filled with meaning and learning.

Praised are you, Adonai our God, for the privilege of writing and editing this Seder, for friends, family and colleagues who helped me, and for the graciousness of Your presence which is with me each day.

Adam Fisher
Stony Brook, New York
25 Sivan 5749
June 28, 1989

SEDER I

TREES

Winter is still with us. Nature seems asleep.
The trees stand with black and brown branches
against the pale winter sky.
In the Land of Israel
spring is almost here.
Flowers begin to dot the fields,
almond trees begin to blossom.
Heavy winter rains are over,
gentler showers fall;
sap begins to rise in trees.

Jews there and here and everywhere
celebrate Tu BiShevat, a new year for trees.

On Tu BiShevat our ancestors
looked forward to the pink flowers of spring,
the red and yellow fruit of summer,
when they would bring gifts to the Temple
and provide for the poor.

We too rejoice at the renewal of life,
and thank God for the blessings of branch and bud.

𝄞 Hinei Ma Tov p. 74

הִנֵּה מַה־טּוֹב וּמַה־נָּעִים
שֶׁבֶת אַחִים גַּם־יָחַד.

Hi-nei ma tov u-ma na-im
she-vet a-chim gam ya-chad.

Behold, how good and how pleasant it is for people to be together.

3

The Original Tu BiShevat

With new buds formed and new rains falling, Tu BiShevat was the new year for tithing fruit which the trees would soon bear. A tenth of the produce was brought to the Temple, and every third year it was given to the poor. It was given in recognition that God is the source of all blessings:

"Every year, you shall set aside a tenth part of the yield, so that you may learn to revere your God forever."
(Deuteronomy 14.22-23)

Four New Years

The Rabbis taught that there were four new years. The first of Nisan, in the spring, is the new year for kings and feasts —Passover is the first festival. The first of Elul, in late summer, is the new year for tithing animals born that year. The first of Tishri, our Rosh Hashana, is the new year for counting the passage of years. The fifteenth of Shevat, Tu BiShevat, is the new year for tithing the first fruit of fruit trees.

(Mishnah Rosh Hashana 1.1)

Why The Trees' New Year is in Shevat

What is the reason that the New Year for tithing trees is in Shevat? By then, most of the rainy season has passed and the sap has risen; but the time of ripening has not yet begun.

(Rosh Hashana 14a with Rashi)

Names for Tu BiShevat

Tu BiShevat is shorthand for the Hebrew Chamisha Asar BiShevat, the fifteenth of Shevat. This day is also called "Chag Hailanot, Festival of Trees" and "Chag Ha-peirot, Festival of Fruit."

The New Year for Trees

All year
They have kept a careful record
Of everything
The waters of the moon
The slow descent
Of every sun
All year
They have charted the course
of every comet
Eyes drawn to the center
To the star that supports
The planet
The beam that holds up every arch
The line that continues into the future
Unbroken
Unchanged.

But tonight
As the light descends into sleep
The trees
All lift their branches to the sky
Cradling the moon
That shines through the night
Like blossoms of the almond
That have already appeared
To announce
That all fruit that follows
Belongs to the new year
To come.

(Howard Schwartz)

Sephardic Customs

Sephardic Jews call this day "Frutas, the Feast of Fruits" or "Rosasana dos Arbores, Rosh Hashana of the Trees."
In Morocco, the rich invite the poor to fill their hats with fruit.
In Safed the Kabbalists celebrated a special seder.

Modern Israel

Since our people have returned to the land we have drained the swamps and planted forests on the mountains, grain in the valleys and flowers in the desert.
On Tu BiShevat, Israel celebrates by planting trees.

(When many children are present:)
Tu BiShevat Is a Birthday
Every person has a birthday.
Every year has a birthday — Rosh Hashana.
Every tree has a birthday too.

Today is the birthday for trees.
This day is called Tu BiShevat.

It is still cold outside
but now, after their winter rest,
the trees begin to grow again.
They draw water from the ground
into their roots
and sap begins to flow
into their branches.
In a few weeks
we will see their leaves and flowers.
In a few months they will give us their fruit.

Today we celebrate their birthday.
Today is the birthday for trees.

Winter Air
A small green spruce
struggles through gray brush,
near the shadow
of a winter-dead oak,
and suns itself,
while gently swaying
to the air of God's love.
(Adam Fisher)

Fifteenth of Shevat
On the fifteenth of Shevat
when spring comes,
an angel descends, ledger in hand,
and enters each bud, each twig, each tree,
and all our garden flowers.
From town to town, from village to village
he makes his winged way,
searching the valleys, inspecting the hills,

flying over the desert
and returns to heaven.
And when the ledger will be full
of trees and blossoms and shrubs,
when the desert is turned into a meadow
and all our land is a watered garden,
the messiah will appear.
(Sh. Shalom)

Song of Songs
Arise my love, my fair one,
and come away;
for lo, the winter is past.
Flowers appear on the earth,
the time of singing is here.
The song of the dove
is heard in our land.
Let us go down to the vineyards
to see if the vines have budded.
There will I give you my love.
(Song of Songs 2.10-12; 7.12)

 ## Nitzanim Niru p. 75

נִצָּנִים נִרְאוּ בָאָרֶץ
עֵת זָמִיר הִגִּיעַ
כִּי־הִנֵּה סְתָו עָבָר
סְתָו חָלַף הָלַךְ לוֹ
הַגְּפָנִים סְמָדַר
נָתְנוּ רֵיחָם

Nit-sa-nim nir-u ba-a-rets
eit za-mir hi-gi-a, eit za-mir. (2x)
Ki hi-nei se-tav a-var,
se-tav cha-laf ha-lach lo
ha-ge-fa-nim se-ma-dar
na-te-nu na-te-nu rei-cham.

Buds are seen in the land
the time of singing has come.
Fall has passed; the vines are blooming,
giving their scent.
(Song of Songs 2)

5

CREATION

On this day, when we celebrate the renewal of trees, we remember that God created all plants and trees. Then, "God said, 'See, I give you every seed-bearing plant that is upon all the earth, and every tree that is upon all the earth, and every tree that has seed-bearing fruit; they shall be yours for food.' And it was so."

And God saw all that was done, and found it very good.

(Genesis 1.29-31)

(When many children are present.)
This is Very Good p. 96
When God made the world,
and made it full of light;
the sun to shine by day,
the moon and stars by night.
You made it full of life:
lilies, oaks, and trout,
tigers and bears,
sparrows, hawks, and apes.

And God took clay
from earth's four corners
to give it the breath of life.
And God said:

This is very good! (2x)

Man, woman, and child.
All are good.
Man, woman, and child
Resemble God.

Like God, we love.
Like God, we think.
Like God we care. (2x)

Man, woman, and child.
All are good.

Blessings for Creation

Master of the universe,
grant us the ability to be alone:
may it be our custom to go outdoors each day
among the trees and grass,
among all growing things,
and there may we be alone,
and enter into prayer.

There may we express all that is in our hearts,
talking with the One to whom we belong.
And may all grasses, trees, and plants
awake at our coming.

Send the power of their life
into our words of prayer,
making whole our hearts and our speech.

(Rabbi Nachman of Bratzlav)

(Choose one of the following series of blessings:)

1. Blessings

בָּרוּךְ אַתָּה, יְיָ אֱלֹהֵינוּ, מֶלֶךְ הָעוֹלָם, עֹשֶׂה מַעֲשֵׂה בְרֵאשִׁית.

Ba-ruch a-ta, A-do-nai E-lo-hei-nu, me-lech ha-o-lam, o-seh ma-a-sei ve-rei-shit.

We praise You, Adonai our God, Creator of the universe, who continually
does the work of creation.

בָּרוּךְ אַתָּה, יְיָ אֱלֹהֵינוּ, מֶלֶךְ הָעוֹלָם, שֶׁכָּכָה לוֹ בְּעוֹלָמוֹ.

Ba-ruch a-ta, A-do-nai E-lo-hei-nu, me-lech ha-o-lam, she-ka-cha lo be-o-la mo.

We praise You, Adonai our God, Ruler of the universe, whose world is filled with
beauty.

בָּרוּךְ אַתָּה, יְיָ אֱלֹהֵינוּ, מֶלֶךְ הָעוֹלָם, שֶׁלֹּא חִסַּר בְּעוֹלָמוֹ דָּבָר, וּבָרָא בּוֹ
בְּרִיּוֹת טוֹבוֹת וְאִילָנוֹת טוֹבִים לְהַנּוֹת בָּהֶם בְּנֵי אָדָם.

Ba-ruch a-ta, A-do-nai E-lo-hei-nu, me-lech ha-o-lam, she-lo chi-sar ba-o-lam da-
var, u-va-ra vo be-ri-ot to-vot ve-i-la-not to-vim le-ha-not ba-hem be-nei a-dam.

We praise You, Adonai our God, Creator of the universe. Your world lacks
nothing needful; You have fashioned goodly creatures and lovely trees that
enchant the heart.

7

2. Blessings of Pleasure

Skin-soft dogwood petals
white cherry clusters
pink nectarine blossoms
magenta wygelia
yellow forsythia sprays

I praise You
who placed such beauty
in Your world.

Smelling
scrub oak and birch woods
spongy mulch
pungent after a rain,
pitch pines on sandy barrens
tang of juniper berries

I praise You
for creating fragrant woods.

Heavy scented lilacs
cut roses in a vase,

lemon balm lavender
summer marigolds
my hands after picking tomatoes,

I praise You
for creating fragrant plants.

Ginger tarragon cinnamon fennel
sweet basil marjoram cumin cloves,

I praise You
for creating piquant spices.

Soft smooth cream colored banana
red raspberries full of seeds
a section of naval orange,
juice on my chin,
cold grapes
plucked from the stem,

I praise You
who creates luscious fruit.

(Adam Fisher)

A Psalm for You

For cool breezes that dance and float
over budding trees,
we bless You.
For lilac buds, and buds on tulips,
for fragrance of lemon balm and mint,
for hosta and lily and iris shoots,
for flowers: daffodils and violet vinca,
grape hyacinth and forsythia,
which sing in early sun,
which sway under clear skies,
which leap through shadows
on warming ground,
we sing Your praises.

And the doves, the doves coo and call,
cardinals whistling back and forth,
grackles with iridescent heads,
swans, a dozen pair in an inlet—
For these and all wonders,
for new-found hope and joy
and gratitude itself,
do we praise You. Halleluya!
(Adam Fisher)

Winter Prayer

The trees have just been washed
   scrubbed clean
by January rain.
Maple bark
   dark brown and light
   gray and tan
black pines
all stand out clearly
   against a mottled sky.
Praised are You, the Holy one
who daily renews creation.
(Adam Fisher)

From Psalm 104

Praise God, O my Soul;
My God, You are very great;

You are clothed in glory and majesty,
wrapped in a robe of light.

You spread the heavens like a tent cloth.

You set the rafters of Your lofts in
the waters.
You make the clouds of Your chariot
move on the wings of the wind.

The trees of the Holy One drink their fill,
the cedars of Lebanon, God's own
planting,

Where birds make their nests;
the stork has her home in the junipers.

From Psalm 148

Halleluya.
Praise the Holy One from the heavens;
praise God on high.

Praise the Holy One, O you who are
on earth,
all sea monsters and ocean depths,

Fire and hail, snow and smoke,
storm wind that execute God's command,

All mountains and hills,
all fruit trees and cedars.

Let them praise the name of God,
   for God's name alone is sublime;
   the splendor of the Holy One
   covers heaven and earth.

9

𝄞 **Eili, Eili** p. 76

אֵלִי, אֵלִי,
שֶׁלֹּא יִגָּמֵר לְעוֹלָם
הַחוֹל וְהַיָּם,
רִשְׁרוּשׁ שֶׁל הַמַּיִם,
בְּרַק הַשָּׁמַיִם,
תְּפִלַּת הָאָדָם.

Ei-li, Ei-li,
she-lo yi-ga-meir le-o-lam:
ha-chol ve-ha-yam,
rish-rush shel ha-ma-yim,
be-rak ha-sha-mayim,
te-fi-lat ha-a-dam. (2x)

O God, our God,
We pray that these things
never end:
The sand and the sea,
The rush of the waters,
The crash of the heavens,
The prayer of the heart. (2x)

(Hannah Senesh)

(On Shabbat:)

Lighting Shabbat Candles

We are more than just hands and minds.
We are people who need time
to see the beauty of God's world,
to appreciate the wonder of life.

On Shabbat we celebrate God's creation.
We rejoice in the work of the Holy One.

בָּרוּךְ אַתָּה, יְיָ אֱלֹהֵינוּ, מֶלֶךְ הָעוֹלָם, אֲשֶׁר קִדְּשָׁנוּ בְּמִצְוֹתָיו וְצִוָּנוּ לְהַדְלִיק
נֵר שֶׁל שַׁבָּת.

Ba-ruch a-ta, A-do-nai E-lo-hei-nu, me-lech ha-o-lam, a-sher
ki-de-sha-nu be-mits-vo-tav ve-tsi-va-nu le-had-lik neir shel Sha-bat.
We praise You, Adonai our God, Ruler of the universe, who hallows us
with mitzvot, and commands us to kindle the lights of Shabbat.

10

(On weekdays and Shabbat:)

The First Cup:
White Wine — The Renewal of Trees

On this way-station
between the bleak white winter
when the trees' sap begins to rise,
and the colorful flowers of the warm seasons
when fruits ripen,
we drink four cups of wine,
each one redder than the one before,
each showing that the land becomes warmer,
each one showing that colors of the fruits
deepen as they ripen,
each one in praise of God,
who renews the fruit of trees each year.

Story: The Wagon Driver's Blessing

Rabbi Wolf Zitomirer was an innkeeper in a village. A Jewish wagon driver entered and asked for a glass of wine. When he was about to drink it without reciting a blessing, the Rabbi stopped him and said, "Do you realize the wondrous laws God used to produce the fruit of the soil before it became the drink which you enjoy?" He promptly recited the blessing, and the Rabbi answered, "Amen!"

(Attributed to *Me-orot HaGedolim*)

(On Weekdays:)

בָּרוּךְ אַתָּה, יְיָ אֱלֹהֵינוּ, מֶלֶךְ הָעוֹלָם, בּוֹרֵא פְּרִי הַגָּפֶן.

Ba-ruch a-ta, A-do-nai E-lo-hei-nu, me-lech ha-olam, bo-rei pe-ri ha-ga-fen.
We praise you, Adonai our God, Ruler of the universe, who creates the fruit
of the vine.

(Drink Wine)

(On Shabbat:)

"The heaven and the earth were finished, and all their array. And on the seventh day God finished the work of creation.

And God blessed the seventh day and declared it holy, because on it
God ceased from all the work of creation."

(Genesis 2.1-3)

בָּרוּךְ אַתָּה, יְיָ אֱלֹהֵינוּ, מֶלֶךְ הָעוֹלָם, בּוֹרֵא פְּרִי הַגָּפֶן.

Ba-ruch a-ta, A-do-nai E-lo-hei-nu, me-lech ha-o-lam, bo-rei pe-ri ha-ga-fen.

We praise You, Adonai our God, Ruler of the universe, who creates the fruit of the vine.

בָּרוּךְ אַתָּה, יְיָ אֱלֹהֵינוּ, מֶלֶךְ הָעוֹלָם, אֲשֶׁר קִדְּשָׁנוּ בְּמִצְוֹתָיו וְרָצָה בָנוּ, וְשַׁבַּת
קָדְשׁוֹ בְּאַהֲבָה וּבְרָצוֹן הִנְחִילָנוּ, זִכָּרוֹן לְמַעֲשֵׂה בְרֵאשִׁית. כִּי הוּא יוֹם תְּחִלָּה
לְמִקְרָאֵי קֹדֶשׁ, זֵכֶר לִיצִיאַת מִצְרָיִם. כִּי-בָנוּ בָחַרְתָּ וְאוֹתָנוּ קִדַּשְׁתָּ מִכָּל-הָעַמִּים,
וְשַׁבַּת קָדְשְׁךָ בְּאַהֲבָה וּבְרָצוֹן הִנְחַלְתָּנוּ. בָּרוּךְ אַתָּה, יְיָ, מְקַדֵּשׁ הַשַּׁבָּת.

Ba-ruch a-ta, A-do-nai E-lo-hei-nu, me-lech ha-o-lam a-sher ki-de-sha-nu
be-mits-vo-tav ve-ra-tsa va-nu, ve-Sha-bat kod-sho be-a-ha-va u-ve-ra-tson
hin-chi-la-nu zi-ka-ron le-ma-a-sei ve-rei-shit. Ki hu yom te-chi-la, le-mik-
ra-ei ko-desh zei-cher li-tsi-at Mits-ra-yim. Ki va-nu va-char-ta ve-o-ta-nu
ki-dash-ta mi-kol ha-a-mim, ve-Sha-bat kod-she-cha be-a-ha-va u-ve-ra-tson
hin-chal-ta-nu. Ba-ruch a-ta, A-do-nai, me-ka-deish ha-Sha-bat.

We praise You, Adonai our God, Ruler of the universe, who hallows us with mitzvot and favors us with the holy Shabbat, who lovingly and graciously bestowed upon us a memorial of the act of creation, first of the holy assemblies, a remembrance of the going forth from Egypt. You have chosen us and hallowed us from among all the peoples, by lovingly and graciously bestowing upon us Your holy Sabbath. We praise You, O God, who hallows the Shabbat.

(Drink Wine)

THE LAND — HA-ARETS

We thank You, God, for bright
snow covered branches of winter,
for rain and forests, land and stream,
for the lush trees of summer.

How many things You have made!
You have made them all with wisdom;
the earth is full of Your creation.

(Psalms 104)

We thank You, too, for the Land of Israel as we read: "Your God is bringing you
into a good land, a land with streams and springs and fountains issuing from plain
and hill; a land of wheat and of olive trees and honey; a land of wheat and barley, of
vines, figs, and pomegranates, a land of olive trees and honey; a land where you may
eat food without stint."

(Deuteronomy 8.6-8)

Story: The Trees Choose Israel

When the Holy One created trees, shrubs
and grass, they were invited to choose
where to grow and bloom. Most of them
wanted to grow on great mountains, in lush
quiet valleys. All wanted comfort and honor.
The olive and the fig, the date and the
pomegranate, wheat and barley all had a
different request. "If we have found favor in
Your eyes, plant us in a small dry land." "Why
do you make this request?" asked the
Creator of the world. They answered, "We
have heard that Your people, the people of
Israel, will be given the Land of Israel. It is our
request that we may be permitted to help
the people of Israel make the desert bloom,
cover its fields with wheat and barley, grow
green trees in its mountains and valleys.

Then Israel will find shelter in their shade
and eat from their fruit and dwell in their
land in peace and security."

Story: Each Generation Plants

"When you come into the land you shall
plant..." (Leviticus 19. 23) The Holy one said
to Israel, "Even though you will find the
land full of goodness, don't say, 'We will sit
and not plant.' Rather be careful to plant
trees. Just as you found trees which others
had planted, so you should plant for your
children. No one should say, 'I am old.
How many more years shall I live? Why
should I be troubled for the sake of
others?' Just as he found trees, he should
add more by planting even if he is old."

(*Midrash Tanchuma, Kedoshim* 8)

Even after others destroyed the land,
even after they exiled our people,
we always hoped
that we would live in the land again.

We clung to God's promise
that the land would be restored.

The prophet Amos taught:

I will restore My people Israel.
They shall rebuild ruined cities and inhabit them;
they shall plant vineyards and drink their wine;
they shall till gardens and eat their fruits.
(Amos 9)

The prophet Isaiah taught:

And they shall build the ancient ruins,
raise up the desolations of old,
and renew the ruined cities,
the desolations of many ages.

And God said, "I will plant cedars in the wilderness, acacias and myrtles and oleasters;

I will set cypresses in the desert,
box trees and elms as well —
That all may see and know, consider and comprehend
that the hand of God has created this.
(Isaiah 61 and 41)

The prophet Ezekiel taught:

"I will make the fruit of your trees and the crops of your fields abundant."

And people shall say, "That land, once desolate, has become like the garden of Eden; and cities, once ruined, desolate, and ravaged are now populated and fortified."

The trees of the field shall yield their fruit and the land shall yield its produce.

My people shall continue secure on its own soil. They shall know that I am God when I break the bars of their yoke and rescue them from those who enslaved them.
(Ezekiel 34 and 36)

The vision of the prophets has been fulfilled before our eyes.

The scattered people have been gathered.

The ruined cities have been rebuilt, the land renewed.

Eucalyptus trees have drained the swamps.

Pine trees cover mountains.

Fruits and vegetables grow in the desert.

Israel is renewed

Israel is like the sycamore tree. Even after it is chopped down and its stump is covered with sand for a long time, the sycamore will begin to grow again. So too the Jewish people has made its way through the 'sands' of persecution to flourish in our time.

Redemption

Israel was likened to a tree which stands naked and frozen in winter. Storms cause the tree to sway and threaten to uproot it. Its situation seems to be without any hope. But even at the height of winter, the tree begins to draw renewed life from the depths of the earth. So it is with Israel: they are put to suffering, but in the depths of darkness the light of redemption is ignited.

(Attributed to Rabbi Israel of Tshortokov)

New Life for People and Land

We have gathered up human particles and combined them into the fruitful and creative nucleus of a nation revived. We have built villages and towns, planted gardens and established factories. We have breathed new life into our muted and abandoned ancient language. Such a marvel is unique in the history of human culture.

(Attributed to David Ben Gurion)

Trees in the Land

Let the trees rustle in the summer on the
  mountain,
on the slope of the valleys;
let them fringe the roads
and give shade by day to the wanderer
and shelter to the tired laborer.

(Attributed to Chaim Nachman Bialik)

The Second Cup:
Pink Wine — The Renewal of Israel

Gradually the earth warms and the Land of Israel changes its garment from white to pink as spring flowers appear in the mountains.

בָּרוּךְ אַתָּה, יְיָ אֱלֹהֵינוּ, מֶלֶךְ הָעוֹלָם, בּוֹרֵא פְּרִי הַגָּפֶן.

Ba-ruch a-ta, A-do-nai E-lo-hei-nu, me-lech ha-o-lam, bo-rei pe-ri ha-ga-fen.

We praise You, Adonai our God, Ruler of the universe, who creates the fruit of the vine.

(Drink wine)

♪ Erets Zavat Chalav p. 77

אֶרֶץ זָבַת חָלָב
חָלָב וּדְבַשׁ (4x)
אֶרֶץ זָבַת חָלָב
זָבַת חָלָב וּדְבַשׁ (2x)

E-rets za-vat cha-lav, cha-lav u-de-vash. (4x)

E-rets za-vat cha-lav, za-vat cha-lav u-de-vash. (2x)

"...a land flowing with milk and honey."

(Deuteronomy 11.9)

TORAH — THE TREE OF LIFE

We celebrate the flowering
of Israel's land and people.

We celebrate trees
which nourish our bodies with fruit
and our spirits with beauty.

We celebrate trees, the symbol
of Torah,
called the "Tree of Life."
It nourishes our souls
and enlightens our minds.

We celebrate trees
which convey a sense of long life.

The menora, the symbol of Jewish life,
was patterned after the olive tree
which lives for five hundred or even
two thousand years.

Torah, which is so ancient yet lives today,
is our "Tree of Life."

Torah continues to support and
sustain and renew our lives.

Story: Hold onto Torah
The Gerer Rebbe told this parable: "When a person fell from a boat into the sea, the captain threw him a rope and shouted, 'Take hold of this rope, and do not let go, for if you do you will lose your life.'" The rabbi then remarked, "This story illustrates the verse, 'It (the Torah) is a tree of life to those who take hold of it.' If you let it go, you will lose your life."
(Attributed to *Siach Sarfei Kodesh*)

Story: Torah Crowns this Place
Several rabbis were sitting beneath some trees. One said, "The shade spread over us by these trees is so pleasant! We must crown this place with words of Torah."
(*Zohar, Exodus, Teruma* 127a)

 Eits Chayim p. 78

עֵץ־חַיִּים הִיא לַמַּחֲזִיקִים בָּהּ,
וְתֹמְכֶיהָ מְאֻשָּׁר.
דְּרָכֶיהָ דַרְכֵי־נֹעַם,
וְכָל־נְתִיבוֹתֶיהָ שָׁלוֹם.

Eits cha-yim hi la-ma-cha-zi-kim ba,
ve-to-me-che-ha me-u-shar.
De-ra-che-ha dar-chei no-am,
ve-chol ne-ti-vo-te-ha sha-lom.

It is a tree of life to those who grasp it,
and whoever holds on to it is happy.
Its ways are pleasant ways,
and all its paths, peaceful.

(Proverbs 3.17-18)

THE DIVINE TREE OF LIFE

The fruit which nourishes life
comes from the trees of God's earth.

Torah, which is a Tree of Life,
comes from our covenant with God.

The flow of life and energy from God
was pictured by the Kabbalists
as coming through the Divine Tree,
another "Tree of Life," as they called it.
This Divine Tree of Life is inverted;
its roots are in the heavens with God,
invisible, inexplicable, unknowable,
yet its branches stretch down toward us
bringing the flow of God's energy
which creates, shapes, and gives life to our world.

We celebrate the trees which give us fruit.
We celebrate Torah, the Tree of life,
which nourishes the spirit.

On Tu BiShevat we celebrate the Divine Tree of Life,
and the renewal of the flow of God's creative power and energy
into our world.

FRUIT OF GOD'S EARTH

Our God, we voice our praise
for the world You have created,
for the land of our people restored,
for Torah which nourishes our souls.

We now enjoy the fruits of Your world
with words of thanks and songs of joy.

Creator of all worlds, the flow of Your spirit
makes all plants sprout, all trees bud.

We praise You on this day for forming buds
that bring luscious fruit.

May it be Your will, Adonai our God,
that as we eat this fruit with love for You,
acknowledging Your greatness, and singing Your praises,
Your power will cause buds to form,
beautiful flowers and ripe fruit to grow in abundance
for good and for blessing.

May the land give its plenty
and the trees of the field give their fruit.

(Based on *Peri Ets Hadar*)

Fruit with Shells

Nuts, Etrogs, Pomegranates, Oranges, Grapefruit

(Read the passage on Kabbala and/or a passage for at least one fruit with shells.)

Kabbala

One level of God's creation is the physical world called *asiya*, the world we know when we use God's gifts to make things. Here, in wood and branch, the spirit, the Divine Spark, is hidden by the shell of its appearance. Fruit, like nuts, with their hard outer shells, remind us that God's presence is often hidden. And, when we eat them with reverence for their beauty and the goodness of their Creator, we become aware of the Divine source of their renewal.

When we say words of praise and thanks to God with kavana, with devotion, we pierce the shell over our own souls and find the Divine sparks in ourselves.

The shell which conceals also protects. In the world of work, of everyday activity, the spiritual requires protection and nurturing. Special effort is necessary to protect it from indifference, from being forgotten, from unkind influences.

When we say words of praise and thanks to God, with kavana, with devotion, for hard-shelled fruit, we remove its protective covering and release the Divine sparks in ourselves and in the world.

Almonds and Other Nuts

The First to Awaken

The almond tree has special significance for Tu BiShevat. The word for almond in Hebrew means to "watch" or "wake." The almond tree is among the first to awaken out of its winter sleep and by the fifteenth of

Shevat it is already full of blossoms, the blooms of fruitful promise.

I said to the almond tree, "Sister, speak to me of God," and the almond tree blossomed.
(Attributed to N. Kazantzakis)

Hashekeidiya p. 79

הַשְׁקֵדִיָּה פּוֹרַחַת

וְשֶׁמֶשׁ פָּז זוֹרַחַת.

צִפֳּרִים מֵרֹאשׁ כָּל גַּג

מְבַשְּׂרוֹת אֶת בֹּא הֶחָג.

טוּ בִּשְׁבָט הִגִּיעַ חַג הָאִילָנוֹת (2x)

Ha-she-kei-di-ya po-ra-chat,
ve-she-mesh paz zo-ra-chat.
Tsi-po-rim mei-rosh kol gag,
me-va-se-rot et bo he-chag.
Tu Bi-Shevat hi-gi-a, chag ha-il-a-not. (2x)

The almond tree is blooming
'neath the golden sun.
Birds sing from every roof
telling us the time has come.
Tu BiShevat has come, the holiday of trees.

Story: Israel and Walnuts

Rabbi Tarfon likened the people of Israel to a pile of walnuts. If one walnut is removed, each and every walnut in the pile will be shaken.

When a single Jew is in trouble, every other Jew is shaken and affected.
(Avot DeRabbi Natan 18.1)

Always a Jew

Why is Israel likened to a nut? The walnut cannot smuggle itself through customs but rattles and is caught. A Jew cannot walk undetected, but wherever he goes, even if he denies it, he is identified as a Jew.
(Song of Songs Rabba 6.11)

Israel, the Branch and the Tree

An Israelite in her relationship to the synagogue may be likened to a branch growing on a tree. As long as the branch is still attached to the tree, there is hope it may renew its vigor no matter how withered it has become; but, once the living branch falls away all hope is lost.
(Attributed to Or Yesharim)

Tzedaka

There are three types of nuts. There are nuts that can be cracked by hand; there are nuts that you have to strike in order to crack them; and there are nuts that are impossible to crack. In the same way, there are Jews who give tzedaka willingly, Jews who will give if you press them, and Jews who will not give even when

Pomegranates

In the Song of Songs we read: "And the pomegranates were in flower." The Rabbis comment: "These are the children who are busy learning the Torah; they sit in rows like pomegranate seeds."

Children are the crowns of the Torah, adorning it just as silver rimmonim,
pomegranates, adorn the top of the Torah Scroll.

(*Song of Songs Rabba* 6.11)

El Ginat Egoz p. 80

אֶל גִּנַּת אֱגוֹז יָרַדְתִּי,
לִרְאוֹת בְּאִבֵּי הַנָּחַל,
לִרְאוֹת הֲפָרְחָה הַגֶּפֶן,
הֵנֵצוּ הָרִמּוֹנִים.

El gi-nat e-goz ya-ra-de-ti,
lir-ot be-i-bei ha-na-chal,
lir-ot ha-pa-re-cha ha-ge-fen,
he-ne-tzu ha-ri-mo-nim.

I went down to the nut garden,
to see the young plants
growing by the stream,
to see if the vine has blossomed,
if the pomegranate has bloomed.
(Song of Songs 6.11)

Eits Rimon p. 81

עֵץ הָרִמּוֹן נָתַן רֵיחוֹ,
בֵּין יַם הַמֶּלַח עַד יְרִיחוֹ.
שָׁב חוֹמָתִי, גְּדוּדֵךְ מִנְּדוֹד,
שָׁב, תַּמָּתִי, דּוֹדֵךְ מִדּוֹד.

Eits ha-ri-mon na-tan rei-cho
bein yam ha-me-lach ad Ye-ri-cho.
Shav, cho-ma-ti, ge-du-deich mi-ne-dod,
shav, ta-ma-ti, do-dech mi-dod.

The pomegranate tree gives of its
fragrance.

Etrog

The etrog is unique. The blossom end does not drop off after pollination
as with other fruit. For this reason the etrog became a symbol of fertility.
It has become customary to preserve it with cloves and save it from
Sukkot until now. Some use it each week for the Havdala service at the
end of Shabbat.

בָּרוּךְ אַתָּה, יְיָ אֱלֹהֵינוּ, מֶלֶךְ הָעוֹלָם, בּוֹרֵא מִינֵי בְשָׂמִים.

Ba-ruch a-ta, A-do-nai E-lo-hei-nu, me-lech ha-o-lam, bo-rei mi-nei ve-sa-mim.

We praise You, Adonai our God, Ruler of the universe, who creates all
spices.

(Pass the etrog and enjoy its fragrance.)

21

Etrog and Israel
Just as the etrog provides both
nourishment and fragrance, so in Israel
there are people who provide both
wisdom and do good deeds.
(*Vayikra Rabba* 30.12)

Blessing on Eating Fruit

The first kind of fruit we taste has a shell which cannot be eaten. This
shell protects the fruit inside, just as a baby is protected inside its
mother's womb or as a young child is protected by its parents.

בָּרוּךְ אַתָּה, יְיָ אֱלֹהֵינוּ, מֶלֶךְ הָעוֹלָם, בּוֹרֵא פְּרִי הָעֵץ.

Ba-ruch a-ta, A-do-nai E-lo-hei-nu, me-lech ha-o-lam, bo-rei pe-ri ha-eits.
We praise you You, Adonai our God, Ruler of the universe, who creates
the fruit of the tree.

בָּרוּךְ אַתָּה, יְיָ אֱלֹהֵינוּ, מֶלֶךְ הָעוֹלָם, שֶׁהֶחֱיָנוּ וְקִיְּמָנוּ וְהִגִּיעָנוּ לַזְּמַן הַזֶּה.

Ba-ruch a-ta, A-do-nai E-lo-hei-nu, me-lech ha-o-lam, she-he-che-ya-nu,
ve-ki-ye-ma-nu ve-hi-gi-a-nu la-ze-man ha-zeh.

We praise You, Adonai our God, Ruler of the universe, for giving us life,
for sustaining us, and for enabling us to reach this season.

(Enjoy nuts and other fruit with shells.)

Fruit with Pits
Dates, Olives, Apricots, Peaches, Plums/Prunes
(Read the passage on Kabbala and/or a passage on at least one kind of fruit with pits.)

Kabbala

God is the creator not only of the physical world we use, but also of our ability to be creative, our capacity to feel, speak and sing.

God is the source of the artist's eye, the musician's ear, the One who inspires the poet's soul.

The Kabbalists called this the world of *yetsira* or formation. When we eat fruit containing pits we are reminded that despite all the wondrous expressions of the human spirit, and our efforts to express God's Presence, we are still, deep inside, tied to the world, part of the natural cycles of life and death. Here, the human spirit is disclosed, yet the Divine Spark must still be protected from within.

When we say praises to God before we eat fruit containing pits, we thank the Source of all life, for expressions of the human spirit; and we acknowledge our limitations before our Creator.

Date Palm
Israel Is Like a Date Palm

The date palm *(tamar)* abounds in blessing, for every part of it can be used, every part is needed. Its dates are for eating, its branches are for blessing on Sukkot; its fronds are for thatching; its fibers are for ropes; its webbing for sieves; its thick trunks for building.

So it is with Israel: each community, each person, plays its part in serving God.
(*Numbers Rabba* 3.1)

23

Tsadik Katamar p. 82

Tsa-dik ka-ta-mar yif-rach,

ke-e-rets ba-Le-va-non yis-geh.

She-tu-lim be-veit A-do-nai,

be-chats-rot E-lo-hei-nu yaf-ri-chu.

Od ye-nu-vun be-sei-va,

de-shei-nim ve-ra-a-na-nim yih-yu,

le-ha-gid ki ya-shar A-do-nai,

tsu-ri ve-lo av-la-ta bo.

צַדִּיק כַּתָּמָר יִפְרָח

כְּאֶרֶז בַּלְּבָנוֹן יִשְׂגֶּה.

שְׁתוּלִים בְּבֵית יְיָ,

בְּחַצְרוֹת אֱלֹהֵינוּ יַפְרִיחוּ.

עוֹד יְנוּבוּן בְּשֵׂיבָה,

דְּשֵׁנִים וְרַעֲנַנִּים יִהְיוּ,

לְהַגִּיד כִּי־יָשָׁר יְיָ,

צוּרִי וְלֹא־עַוְלָתָה בּוֹ.

The righteous shall bloom like a date palm;

they thrive like a cedar in Lebanon;

planted in the house of God,

they flourish in the courts of our Creator.

(Psalms 92)

Two Date Palm Trees

Once upon a time there was a date palm in Jericho which bore no fruit. One day a date grower passed by and said, "This date palm longs for a certain date palm near Jericho. She longs with all her heart." The grower went to that tree and brought pollen to pollinate the flowers so that she might produce lovely clusters of dates.

(*Numbers Rabba* 3.1)

Olive Tree
Hope for all

The olive tree is a sign of hope that life can be restored. When the great flood began to subside, Noah sent out a dove. "The dove came back to him toward evening, and there in its bill was a leaf it had picked from an olive tree."

(Genesis 8.11)

Hope for Israel

The prophet Hosea taught that the olive tree is a sign of future hope about Israel. God promises:

"Its boughs shall spread out far, its beauty shall be like the olive tree's, its fragrance like that of Lebanon."

(Hosea 14.7)

Israel Not Lost

Rabbi Joshua ben Levi said, "Why is Israel likened to an olive tree? To tell you that just as the olive tree does not lose its leaves either in summer or in winter, so Israel shall never be lost either in this world or in the world to come."

(Menachot 53b)

(One of the following may be sung:)

Atsei Zeitim p. 83

עֲצֵי זֵיתִים עוֹמְדִים.

A-tsei zei-tim om-dim.

Olive trees are standing.

Jerusalem of Gold p. 84

The olive trees that stand in silence
Upon the hills of time,
To hear the voices of the city
As bells of evening chime.
The shofar sounding from the temple
To call the world to prayer,
The shepherd pauses in the valley
And peace is everywhere.

Chorus

יְרוּשָׁלַיִם שֶׁל זָהָב
וְשֶׁל נְחשֶׁת וְשֶׁל אוֹר
הֲלֹא לְכָל שִׁירַיִךְ
אֲנִי כִּנּוֹר

Ye-ru-sha-la-yim shel za-hav
Ve-shel ne-cho-shet ve-shel or,
Ha-lo le-chol shi-ra-yich
A-ni ki-nor.

The water well for those who thirsted,
The ancient market square;
Your golden sun that lights the future
For all those everywhere.
How many songs, how many stories
The stony hills recall,
Around her heart my city carries
A lonely ancient wall.

Chorus

And far away beyond the desert
A thousand suns will glow;
We shall be going to the Jordan
By way of Jericho.
My simple voice cannot acclaim thee,
Too weak the words I choose.
Jerusalem, if I forget thee,
May my right hand its cunning lose.

Chorus

25

Blessing on Eating Fruit

The second kind of fruit we taste has a hard pit inside and its fruit on the outside.

בָּרוּךְ אַתָּה, יְיָ אֱלֹהֵינוּ, מֶלֶךְ הָעוֹלָם, בּוֹרֵא פְּרִי הָעֵץ.

Ba-ruch a-ta, A-do-nai E-lo-hei-nu, me-lech ha-o-lam bo-rei pe-ri ha-eits.

We praise You, Adonai our God, Ruler of the universe, who creates the fruit of the tree.

(Enjoy fruit such as olives and dates.)

Entirely Edible Fruit
Figs, Raisins, Strawberries, Apples, Pears, Carob

(Read the passage on Kabbala and/or a passage on at least one kind of entirely edible fruit.)

Kabbala

While we can participate in the first two aspects of creation, using things and creating works of art, only God is the creator of all.

And it is only with God that all barriers between the physical and the spiritual are eliminated.

This world, called *beri-a,* is echoed in our dreams and thoughts in which the barriers of the spiritual and physical are blurred.

This is represented by fruit such as raisins and figs in which the seeds and the fruit are interspersed.

When we say praises to God before eating this fruit, we acknowledge a world so close to God that there are no barriers, and the spark of the Divine flows freely.

Figs

Symbols of Peace

The Bible speaks of the fig tree in a time of peace when "They shall beat their swords into plowshares and their spears into pruning hooks.
Nation shall not take up
sword against nation;
they shall never again know war.

But all shall sit
under their grapevine or fig tree
with no one to disturb them."

(Micah 4.3-4)

♪ Lo Yisa Goi p. 86

לֹא יִשָּׂא גוֹי אֶל גוֹי חֶרֶב,
לֹא יִלְמְדוּ עוֹד מִלְחָמָה.

Lo yi-sa goi el goi che-rev,
lo yil-me-du od mil-cha-ma.

Nation shall not take up
sword against nation;
they shall never again know war.

(Micah 4.3)

♪ Veyashvu Ish p. 87

וְיָשְׁבוּ אִישׁ תַּחַת גַּפְנוֹ
וְתַחַת תְּאֵנָתוֹ
וְאֵין מַחֲרִיד

Ve-ya-she-vu ish ta-chat gafe-no
ve-ta-chat te-ei-na-to
ve-ein ma-cha-rid.

They shall sit, everyone under their grapevine or fig tree with no one to disturb them.

(Micah 4.4)

Fig Tree and Torah

The rabbis asked, "Why were the words of Torah compared to the fig tree?"

They answered, "Since all the figs do not ripen at the same time, the more one searches the tree, the more figs one finds in it."

So it is with the words of the Torah: the more we study them, the more delight we take in them.

(Eruvin 54a)

All of Torah Is Good

Why is the Torah compared to a fig? Because nearly every fruit has some part which cannot be eaten: dates have pits, grapes have seeds, pomegranates have skin. But every part of the fig is good to eat.
(Yalkut Shimoni, Joshua 1)

Story: Plant for the Future

Once an old man was planting a fig tree when a Roman general happened to pass by. He laughed at the old man and said, "You Jews are stupid. Don't you realize it will take twenty years before that tree will grow enough to give fruit, and you will be long dead by then."

The old man answered, "When I was a small child I could eat fruit because those who came before me had planted trees. Am I not obliged to do the same for the next generation?"

The general responded, "If you are privileged to eat of them, let me know." In the course of time the trees produced figs, and the old man lived long enough to enjoy them. He filled a basket and brought them to the general who honored him.

The general's servants were surprised that he would show honor to a Jew, but the general told them, "His Creator honors him, and shall I not honor him too?"

(Leviticus Rabba 25.5)

 **Ki Tavo-u** p. 88

וְכִי תָבוֹאוּ אֶל הָאָרֶץ,
וּנְטַעְתֶּם כָּל עֵץ תְּחִלָּה.
וְנָתַן הָעֵץ פִּרְיוֹ
וְהָאָרֶץ יְבוּלָהּ.
עֵת לִנְטוֹעַ אִילָנוֹת.

Ki ta-vo-u el ha-a-rets
u-ne-ta-a-tem kol eits te-chi-la.
Ve-na-tan ha-eits pir-yo
ve-ha-a-rets ye-vu-la.
Eit lin-to-a i-la-not. (3x)

When you come to the land and plant trees, each tree shall give its fruit and the land shall give its abundance. It is time to plant trees.

Carob

The carob has a special place in Jewish life because during the war with Rome, our people lived under a siege and managed to survive by eating the fruit of the carob tree.

The Hebrew words for carob (*charuv*), sword (*cherev*), and destruction (*churban*) are all similar. They remind us of the war and the destruction of the Temple. The carob is even shaped like a sword.

Blessing on Eating Fruit

The third kind of fruit we taste is entirely edible.

בָּרוּךְ אַתָּה, יְיָ אֱלֹהֵינוּ, מֶלֶךְ הָעוֹלָם, בּוֹרֵא פְּרִי הָעֵץ.

Ba-ruch a-ta, A-do-nai E-lo-hei-nu, me-lech ha-o-lam bo-rei pe-ri ha-eits. We praise You, Adonai our God, Ruler of the universe, who creates the fruit of the tree.

(Enjoy fruit such as figs, raisins, strawberries, apples, pears, carob.)

The Source of All Fruit

When we think of all that we have tasted,

When we remember all that we have enjoyed,

Our hearts and minds are directed to the Holy One,

The Holy One who is beyond all understanding,

The source of life whose reality we cannot know,

The source of all that we have and see,

The source of the flow of life which gives new life to all trees, and ripens all fruit.

Kabbala—The Ineffable World

This is the world of God, in which there is no physical representation and in which only God's eternal qualities reside. It is the ineffable world called *atsilut*, or emanation

The Third Cup:
Light Red Wine — Israel's Spring Fruit

In the Land of Israel, the first spring fruits ripen — strawberries, melons and apricots; red poppies and tulips cover the ground like a blanket, brightening the countryside.

בָּרוּךְ אַתָּה, יְיָ אֱלֹהֵינוּ, מֶלֶךְ הָעוֹלָם, בּוֹרֵא פְּרִי הַגָּפֶן.

Ba-ruch a-ta, A-do-nai El-o-hei-nu, me-lech ha-o-lam, bo-rei pe-ri ha-ga-fen.
We praise You, Adonai our God, Ruler of the world, who creates the fruit of the vine.

(Drink wine.)

♪ **Havu Lanu Yayin** p. 89

הָבוּ לָנוּ יַיִן, יַיִן
לֹא שָׁתִינוּ עוֹד עֲדַיִן
הָבוּ לָנוּ יַיִן, וְתִירוֹשׁ.

Ha-vu la-nu ya-yin, ya-yin,
lo sha-ti-nu od a-da-yin.
Ha-vu la-nu ya-yin ve-ti-rosh.

Give us wine,
for we have not sipped it yet.
Give us wine to drink.

A FESTIVE MEAL

Washing the Hands
We wash our hands in water
which sustains our lives,
the life of trees,
and all life.

We wash our hands in water
which cleanses and purifies,
preparing us for the holiness of blessing,

The holiness of eating of God's bounty
with *kavana*, devotion,
and *deveikut*, closeness to God.

בָּרוּךְ אַתָּה, יְיָ אֱלֹהֵינוּ, מֶלֶךְ הָעוֹלָם,
אֲשֶׁר קִדְּשָׁנוּ בְּמִצְוֹתָיו וְצִוָּנוּ עַל-
נְטִילַת יָדָיִם.

Ba-ruch a-ta, A-do-nai E-lo-hei-nu, me-lech
ha-o-lam, a-sher ki-de-sha-nu be-mits-vo-
tav ve-tsi-va-nu al ne-ti-lat ya-da-yim.

We praise You, Adonai our God, Ruler of
the universe, who has made us holy with
Your mitzvot and instructed us concerning
the washing of hands.

Hamotzi

God's rich earth
nurtures wheat and barley,
rye and oats,
and all grains grown for bread:

בָּרוּךְ אַתָּה, יְיָ אֱלֹהֵינוּ, מֶלֶךְ הָעוֹלָם, הַמּוֹצִיא לֶחֶם מִן הָאָרֶץ.
Ba-ruch a-ta, A-donai E-lo-hei-nu, me-lech ha-o-lam ha-mo-tsi le-chem
min ha-a-rets.
We praise You, Adonai our God, Ruler of the universe, who brings forth
bread from the earth.

(Meal is Served)

THANKFULNESS

Thankfulness in Words

(Read one of the following:)

We Praise for Field and Fruit

We praise You our God
for the fruit of the vine,

that we might eat of its fruit
and be satisfied with its goodness.
As it is written:

For the fruits of trees,
for the produce of the field,

"And you shall eat your fill
and praise the name of your God

For the good land You have given
and renewed

who dealt so wondrously with you..."

(Joel 2.26)

God's Gifts

Adonai our God is bringing you into a good land, a land of wheat and
barley, of vines and figs, a land of olive trees and honey;

A land where you may eat food without stint, where you will lack nothing.

When you have eaten your fill, and have built fine houses, and your silver
and gold have increased, beware lest your heart grow haughty and you
forget Adonai, our God, and you say to yourselves, "My own power and
the might of my own hand have won this wealth for me."

Remember, it is God who gives you the power to get wealth.

Therefore when you have eaten your fill give thanks to God for the good
land which has been given to you.

(From Deuteronomy 8)

31

Let All Being Praise God

Praise God, O you who are on the earth,
all sea monsters and ocean depths,
fire and hail, snow and smoke,
storm wind that executes the Creator's
command,
all mountains and hills,
all fruit trees and cedars,
all kings and peoples of the earth,
all princes of the earth and its judges,
youths and maidens alike,
young and old together.

Let them praise the name of God,
whose name alone is sublime;
whose splendor covers heaven and
earth.

(From Psalms 148.7-13)

Fueled

Fueled
by a million
man-made
wings of fire —
the rocket tore a tunnel
through the sky —
and everybody cheered.
Fueled
only by a thought from God —
the seedling
urged its way
through the thickness of black —
and as it pierced
the heavy ceiling of the soil —
up into outer space
no
one
even clapped.

(Marcy Hans)

i thank you God...

i thank you God for this most amazing
day: for the leaping greenly spirits of trees
and a blue true dream of sky; and for
everything
which is natural which is infinite which is yes

(i who have died am alive again today,
and this is the sun's birthday; this is the birth
day of life and of love and wings: and of
the gay
great happening illimitably earth)

how should tasting touching hearing
seeing
breathing, any—lifted from the no
of all nothing—human merely being
doubt unimaginable You?

(now the ears of my ears awake and
now the eyes of my eyes are opened)

(ee cummings)

Story: Which Blessing for a Tree?

A woman was traveling in the desert. She
was hungry, tired and thirsty when she
came to a tree whose fruits were sweet, its
shade was pleasant and a stream of water
flowed beneath it. She ate of its fruit, drank
of the water, and rested under its shade.
When she was about to continue her
journey, she said, "Tree, with what shall I
bless you? Shall I say, 'May your fruit be
sweet?' It is sweet already. Shall I say, 'May
a stream of water flow beneath you?' A
stream of water already flows beneath
you. Shall I say, 'May your shade be
pleasant?' It is already pleasant. Therefore,
I say, 'May it be God's will that all the
shoots taken from you be like you.' "

(*Ta-anit* 5b-6a)

Birkat Hamazon

(On Shabbat begin:)

When the Redeemer restores the exiled of Zion,
we shall be as those who dream.
Our mouths shall be filled with laughter,
our tongues, with songs of joy.

Then will they say among the nations,
"Their God has done great things for them!"

Indeed, God has done great things for us
and we did rejoice.

Restore us once again, O God,
like sudden floodstreams in the Negev.

Then, those who sow in tears
will reap in joy.

Those who go forth weeping,
bearing seed for sowing,
will surely return in joy
carrying their sheaves.

(Psalm 126)

(On Weekdays begin:)

רַבּוֹתַי, נְבָרֵךְ!
Ra-bo-tai ne-va-reich.

יְהִי שֵׁם יְיָ מְבֹרָךְ מֵעַתָּה וְעַד עוֹלָם.
Ye-hi sheim A-do-nai me-vo-rach mei-a-ta ve-ad o-lam.

בִּרְשׁוּת מָרָנָן וְרַבָּנָן וְרַבּוֹתַי, נְבָרֵךְ (אֱלֹהֵינוּ) שֶׁאָכַלְנוּ מִשֶּׁלוֹ.

Bi-re-shut ma-ra-nan ve-ra-ba-nan ve-ra-bo-tai, ne-va-reich (E-lo-hei-nu) she-a-chal-nu mi-she-lo.

בָּרוּךְ (אֱלֹהֵינוּ) שֶׁאָכַלְנוּ מִשֶּׁלוֹ וּבְטוּבוֹ חָיִינוּ.

Ba-ruch (E-lo-hei-nu) she-a-chal-nu mi-she-lo u-ve-tu-vo cha-yi-nu.

Friends, let us praise God.

May God's name be praised now and forever.

Praised is our God of whose abundance
we have eaten.

*Praised is our God of whose abundance
we have eaten and by whose goodness we live.*

בָּרוּךְ אַתָּה, יְיָ, אֱלֹהֵינוּ מֶלֶךְ הָעוֹלָם, הַזָּן אֶת הָעוֹלָם כֻּלּוֹ בְּטוּבוֹ; בְּחֵן בְּחֶסֶד וּבְרַחֲמִים, הוּא נוֹתֵן לֶחֶם לְכָל בָּשָׂר, כִּי לְעוֹלָם חַסְדּוֹ. וּבְטוּבוֹ הַגָּדוֹל תָּמִיד לֹא חָסַר לָנוּ, וְאַל יֶחְסַר לָנוּ מָזוֹן לְעוֹלָם וָעֶד בַּעֲבוּר שְׁמוֹ הַגָּדוֹל; כִּי הוּא אֵל זָן וּמְפַרְנֵס לַכֹּל, וּמֵטִיב לַכֹּל, וּמֵכִין מָזוֹן לְכָל בְּרִיּוֹתָיו אֲשֶׁר בָּרָא. בָּרוּךְ אַתָּה, יְיָ, הַזָּן אֶת הַכֹּל.

Ba-ruch a-ta, A-do-nai E-lo-hei-nu, me-lech ha-o-lam, ha-zan et ha-o-lam ku-lo be-tu-vo be-chein, be-che-sed, u-ve-ra-cha-mim. Hu no-tein le-chem le-chol ba-sar, ki le-o-lam chas-do. U-ve-tu-vo ha-ga-dol ta-mid lo cha-sar la-nu, ve-al ye-che-sar la-nu ma-zon le-o-lam va-ed, ba-a-vur she-mo ha-ga-dol. Ki hu Eil zan u-me-far-neis la-kol u-mei-tiv la-kol u-mei-chin ma-zon le-chol be-ri-yo-tav a-sher ba-ra. Ba-ruch a-ta, A-do-nai, ha-zan et ha-kol.

We praise Adonai our God, Ruler of the universe, whose goodness sustains the world. The God of grace, love, and compassion is the source of food for all who live. Sustenance there is for all. None need ever lack, no being ever want for food. We praise God, the source of food for all life.

34

כַּכָּתוּב: וְאָכַלְתָּ וְשָׂבָעְתָּ, וּבֵרַכְתָּ אֶת יְיָ אֱלֹהֶיךָ עַל הָאָרֶץ הַטֹּבָה אֲשֶׁר נָתַן לָךְ. בָּרוּךְ אַתָּה, יְיָ, עַל הָאָרֶץ וְעַל הַמָּזוֹן.

Ka-ka-tuv, ve-a-chal-ta ve-sa-va-ta, u-vei-rach-ta et A-do-nai E-lo-hei-cha, al ha-a-rets ha-to-va a-sher na-tan lach. Ba-ruch a-ta A-do-nai, al ha-a-rets ve-al ha-ma-zon.

For all these things, Adonai our God, we thank and bless You. As it is written:
"When you have eaten and are satisfied, then praise God who has given you this good land."

We praise You, O God, for the land and for the food.

Our God and God of all ages, be mindful of Your people Israel on this day of Tu BiShevat, and renew in us love and compassion, goodness, life and peace.

This day remember us for well-being.
This day bless us with Your nearness.
This day help us to a fuller life.

Let us all say, *"Amen!"*

וּבְנֵה יְרוּשָׁלַיִם עִיר הַקֹּדֶשׁ בִּמְהֵרָה בְיָמֵינוּ. בָּרוּךְ אַתָּה, יְיָ, בּוֹנֵה בְרַחֲמָיו יְרוּשָׁלָיִם. אָמֵן.

U-ve-nei Ye-ru-sha-la-yim ir ha-ko-desh bi-me-hei-ra be-ya-mei-nu. Ba-ruch a-ta, A-do-nai, bo-neh be-ra-cha-mav Ye-ru-sha-la-yim. A-men.

And build Jerusalem, O God, speedily in our days. We praise You, by whose compassion we will see Jerusalem renewed and at peace. Amen.

(On Shabbat:)

הָרַחֲמָן, הוּא יַנְחִילֵנוּ יוֹם שֶׁכֻּלּוֹ שַׁבָּת וּמְנוּחָה לְחַיֵּי הָעוֹלָמִים:

Ha-ra-cha-man, hu yan-chi-lei-nu yom she-ku-lo sha-bat u-me-nu-cha le-cha-yei ha-o-la-mim.

May the Merciful One favor us with a Shabbat of eternal peace.

May the Merciful One bless this community, and this table at which we have eaten.

(On weekdays continue here:)

עוֹשֶׂה שָׁלוֹם בִּמְרוֹמָיו, הוּא יַעֲשֶׂה שָׁלוֹם עָלֵינוּ וְעַל כָּל יִשְׂרָאֵל. וְאִמְרוּ: אָמֵן.

O-seh sha-lom bi-me-ro-mav, hu ya-a-seh sha-lom a-lei-nu ve-al kol Yis-ra-eil, ve-im-ru: A-men.

May the One who creates harmony throughout nature, bring fulfillment and peace to our world.

יְיָ עֹז לְעַמּוֹ יִתֵּן; יְיָ יְבָרֵךְ אֶת־עַמּוֹ בַשָּׁלוֹם.

A-do-nai oz le-a-mo yi-tein, A-do-nai ye-va-reich et a-mo va-sha-lom.
May God give strength to our people. May God bless us and all peoples with peace.

The Fourth Cup:
Dark Red Wine — The Cup of Thankfulness

In summer the flowers are in full bloom, field and tree yield their fruit. We drink this darkest-red cup of wine in thanks for the richness of God's land.

בָּרוּךְ אַתָּה, יְיָ אֱלֹהֵינוּ, מֶלֶךְ הָעוֹלָם, בּוֹרֵא פְּרִי הַגָּפֶן.

Ba-ruch a-ta, A-do-nai E-lo-hei-nu, me-lech ha-o-lam, bo-rei pe-ri ha-ga-fen.

We praise You, Adonai our God, Ruler of the universe who creates the fruit of the vine.

(Drink Wine)

Thankfulness in Deeds

Tithes

Keren Peirot - Food Fund

"You shall set aside a tenth part of the yield so that the stranger, the fatherless and the widow shall come to eat their fill, and you may learn to revere your God forever."

(From Deuteronomy 14)

We may "eat choice foods and drink sweet drinks" but we should "send portions to those for whom nothing is prepared."

(Nehemiah 8.10)

(Food for the hungry may be provided in several ways: an add-on "tithe" of the cost of the food for the Seder; bringing nourishing non-perishable food items for a local food pantry; an appeal for voluntary contributions, etc.)

Planting

Imitate God

From the very beginning of the creation of the world, the Holy One has been occupied with planting, so when you enter the land, you shall occupy yourself with planting.

(*Leviticus Rabba* 25.3)

Plant for Passover

(Parsley or romaine, which will be used on Passover, can be planted. Prepare a small cup of soil for each family. Parsley or romaine seeds should be provided for planting.)

O God, we thank You for earth and seed; for all things that grow. We rejoice that we might be Your partners in planting. May we celebrate Tu BiShevat, Pesach and all festivals in joy.

(Plant seeds)

🎼 The Planting Song p. 90

There are trees and plants that give us
nearly everything we need,
but don't forget they started out
as tiny little seeds.
You can throw them in the air
or you can hold them in your hand,
but someday those tiny seeds will grow
and trees will fill the land.

Chorus
So take a little seed,
plant it in the ground,
(and that seed will grow as the
seasons flow,
with branches all around.) (2x)

It is written in the Torah,
when we saw the promised land,

we planted trees at every turn,
for this was God's command.
And today in modern Israel,
where they made the desert bloom,
in such a tiny country,
for a tree there's always room.

Chorus

In the Talmud is a saying
written many years ago,
that every plant has a special star
to teach it how to grow.
If you happen to be planting
and someone comes along,
finish what you're doing
and together sing this song.
(Jeffrey Klepper)

Plant Trees in Israel

Our God and God of our fathers and mothers, we are thankful for the renewal of the land of our ancestors. We rejoice that we may have a part in planting forests and making the land blossom. May You bless the land and all its trees with beauty, fruitfulness and peace.

(It is customary to celebrate Tu Bishevat by planting trees in Israel through the Jewish National Fund, the agency responsible for afforestation and land reclamation in Israel. To purchase trees, tree-planting forms can be obtained through your local Jewish National Fund Office.)

Plant for Your Children

"A person's life is sustained by trees. Plant them for the sake of your children."

Planting and Hope

There is a tradition that at the birth of a girl, a cypress tree is planted; and at the birth of a boy, a cedar tree is planted. When a couple is married, they stand under a *chupa* made of wood from the trees planted at their birth.
(*Gittin* 57a)

 ## Turn, Turn, Turn p. 92

Chorus
To everything, turn, turn, turn
There is a season, turn, turn, turn
And a time to every purpose under heaven

A time to be born, a time to die
A time to plant, a time to reap
A time to kill, a time to heal
A time to laugh, a time to weep

Chorus

A time to build up, a time to break down
A time to dance, a time to mourn
A time to cast away stones
A time to gather stones together

Chorus

A time to love, a time to hate
A time of war, a time of peace
A time you may embrace
A time to refrain from embracing

Chorus

A time to gain, a time to lose
A time to rend, a time to sew
A time for love, a time for hate
A time for peace
I swear it's not too late

Chorus
(Pete Seeger, based on Ecclesiastes 3.1-8)

The Messiah

Planting is so important, that if a sapling were in your hand, and you were told that the Messiah had come, first plant the sapling, then go out to greet the Messiah.
(*Avot deRabbi Natan B*, Ch. 31)

The Tree and the Mashi-ach

"If you are planting a tree
and someone comes and says,
'The Mashi-ach is coming!'—
then plant!"
(*Avot deRabbi Natan*)

No matter what reasonable people
or foaming enthusiastic youths tell you:
that this messiah or that messiah
is imminent —
plant!
The Mashi-ach is in no rush.
When you have patted down the last clods
of dirt,
and watered your pines, your cedars,
your gum trees and cypresses,
he will still be wherever he is supposed to be,
and more than happy to admire the sapling
with you.
Messiahs don't come to uproot things.
If he wanted to,
he could bundle Eretz Yisraeil into a
package
and bring it to you,
so you would not have to go wandering
again
through many lands.
If he really is the Mashi-ach,
this One everyone pesters you about,
he can bring you Abraham,
who will sit by your tree
and dispense dates
and the flat bread of hospitality,
as in ancient days.
So plant now, firmly,
and the flat bread of hospitality,
as in ancient days.

So plant now, firmly,
water it well,

whether or not there is a Messiah
today or tomorrow.

(Danny Siegel)

♪ Etein Bamidbar p. 94

אֶתֵּן בַּמִּדְבָּר נֶטַע אֶרֶז,
שִׁטָּה וַהֲדַס וְעֵץ שָׁמֶן,
אָשִׂים בָּעֲרָבָה בְּרוֹשׁ
תִּדְהָר וּתְאַשּׁוּר יַחְדָּיו.

E-tein ba-mid-bar ne-ta e-rez
shi-ta ve-ha-das ve-eits sha-men.
A-sim ba-a-ra-va be-rosh. (2x)

E-tein ba-mid-bar ne-ta e-rez e-rez
shi-ta ve-ha-das ve-eits sha-men sha-men.
A-sim ba-a-ra-va be-rosh,
be-rosh tid-har u-te-a-shur yach-dav.

I will put a cedar plant in the desert,
acacia and myrtle and an oil-producing tree.
I will put a fir tree in the wilderness,
elm and cypress together.

Custodians of God's World

To Tend the World

God took us and placed us in the garden of Eden, to till it and tend it.

(From Genesis 2.15)

Story: Do Not Destroy

The Holy One led Adam through the Garden of Eden and said, "I created all My beautiful and glorious works for your sake. Take heed not to corrupt and destroy My world. For if you corrupt it, there is no one to make it right after you."

(*Ecclesiastes Rabba* 7.13)

Modern pollution

Pesticides and herbicides
forest fires and acid rain
devastation of forests
development of wild lands
erosion of soil
destroy God's land,
despoil our heritage.

Protect Fruit Trees

When in your war against a city you have to besiege it a long time in order to capture it, you must not destroy its trees, wielding the ax against them. You may eat of them, but you must not cut them down. Are trees of the field human, to withdraw before you into the besieged city?

(Deuteronomy 20.19)

When a fruit tree is cut down, its voice goes from one end of the world to the other.

(Pirke DeRabbi Eliezer 34)

Cherry Blossoms

An old woman slowly walks
through the park, admires
a flowering cherry tree,
touches a branch of blossoms,
twists it off leaving
a ragged end. She
carries it home, and leaves it
on the table to die.

(Adam Fisher)

Story: Cain Damages the Ground

There is a very old legend which teaches us that the things people do to one another have an impact on nature. The legend tells us that originally God created each tree so that it could yield many different kinds of fruit. In that way they produced hundreds more different kinds of fruit than we now have. Then a terrible thing happened. Cain killed his brother Abel and the trees went into mourning. They refused to yield their fruit on account of their grief over Abel. Did not God say that the voice of Abel's blood cries out from the ground and that the earth will no longer yield its full strength? From then on each tree would yield just one kind of fruit. Only in the world to come will they return to their full fruitfulness.

(Based on *Midrash Tanchuma*, Buber edition, Introduction 158)

Prayer For Our World

May it be Your will, Adonai our God and God of our fathers and mothers, that all fruit trees be filled with the glory of their buds and blossoms.

May they be renewed each year to grow and yield the fruit of goodness and sweetness.

May we all tend the world You have entrusted to our care.

May we rejoice and share in the fruit of Your earth.

🎼 Hatikva p. 95

כָּל עוֹד בַּלֵּבָב פְּנִימָה
נֶפֶשׁ יְהוּדִי הוֹמִיָּה,
וּלְפַאֲתֵי מִזְרָח קָדִימָה
עַיִן לְצִיּוֹן צוֹפִיָּה.
עוֹד לֹא אָבְדָה תִקְוָתֵנוּ,
הַתִּקְוָה שְׁנוֹת אַלְפַּיִם,
לִהְיוֹת עַם חָפְשִׁי בְּאַרְצֵנוּ,
אֶרֶץ צִיּוֹן וִירוּשָׁלַיִם.

Kol od ba-lei-vav pe-ni-ma
ne-fesh Ye-hu-di ho-mi-ya,
u-le-fa-a-tei miz-rach ka-di-ma
a-yin le-Tsi-yon tso-fi-ya,
od lo av-da tik-va-tei-nu,
ha-tik-va she-not al-pa-yim
(lih-yot am chof-shi be-art-sei-nu
e-rets Tsi-yon vi-Ye-ru-sha-la-yim.) (2x)
So long as still within the inmost heart
a Jewish spirit sings,
so long as the eye looks eastward,
gazing toward Zion,
our hope is not lost —
that hope of two millennia,
to be a free people in our land,
the land of Zion and Jerusalem.

SEDER II

(This Seder is suggested when many children are present.)

TREES

Winter is still with us. Nature seems asleep.
The trees stand with black and brown branches
against the white winter sky.
In the Land of Israel
spring is almost here.
Flowers begin to dot the fields,
almond trees begin to blossom.
Heavy winter rains are over,
lighter showers fall;
sap begins to rise in trees.

Jews there and here and everywhere
celebrate Tu BiShevat, the new year for trees.
We thank God for the renewal of life,
for the blessings of branch and bud.

Hinei Ma Tov p. 74

הִנֵּה מַה־טּוֹב וּמַה־נָּעִים
שֶׁבֶת אַחִים גַּם־יָחַד.

Hi-nei ma tov u-ma na-im
she-vet a-chim gam ya-chad.

Behold, how good and how pleasant it is for people to be together.

45

Tu BiShevat is a Birthday

Every person has a birthday.
Every year has a birthday
called Rosh Hashana.
Every tree has a birthday too.

Today is the birthday for trees.
This day is called Tu BiShevat.

It is still cold outside
but now, after their winter rest,
the trees begin to grow again.

They draw water from the ground
into their roots,
and sap begins to flow
into their branches.
In a few weeks
we will see their leaves and flowers.
In a few months
they will give us their fruit.

Today we celebrate their birthday.
Today is the birthday for trees.

Tu BiShevat p. 98
It's a happy thought
knowing trees are growing.
When it's Tu BiShevat,
nature's praise we're showing.
Think of the clean air
all the trees are making.
Tu BiShevat is here,
time for celebrating.

La, la, la, la...
(Steven Reuben)

46

CREATION

It gave God great joy to create the beautiful world. God created the sky and the earth and oceans and rivers. The ground was ready for trees, flowers and grass, so God made them next.

There were red, red roses and yellow daffodils.

God made the tall trees and many different kinds of food.

There were juicy grapes, sweet purple-plums, red apples and more.

Just think how many different and wonderful tastes there are in this world.

𝄞 This is Very Good p. 96

When God made the world,
and God made it full of light;
the sun to shine by day,
the moon and stars by night.
God made it full of life:
lilies, oaks, and trout,
tigers and bears,
sparrows, hawks, and apes.

And God took clay
from earth's four corners
to give it the breath of life.
And God said:

This is very good! (2x)

Man, woman, and child.
All are good.
Man, woman, and child
Resemble God.

Like God, we love.
Like God, we think.
Like God we care. (2x)

Man, woman, and child.
All are good.

Blessing for Creation

בָּרוּךְ אַתָּה, יְיָ אֱלֹהֵינוּ, מֶלֶךְ הָעוֹלָם, עֹשֶׂה מַעֲשֵׂה בְרֵאשִׁית.

Ba-ruch a-ta, A-do-nai E-lo-hei-nu, me-lech ha-o-lam, o-seh ma-a-sei ve-rei-shit.

We Praise You, Adonai our God, Ruler of the universe, who made our beautiful, wonderful world.

(On Shabbat:)

Lighting Shabbat Candles

We are more than just hands and minds.
We are people who need time
to walk in woods and parks,
to see the snow on pine branches in winter,
to sit in the shade of maples in summer.

On Shabbat we need time
to feel the peace in God's world
and in ourselves.

We light these candles:
they are the lights of peace,
the lights of Sabbath peace.

בָּרוּךְ אַתָּה, יְיָ אֱלֹהֵינוּ, מֶלֶךְ הָעוֹלָם, אֲשֶׁר קִדְּשָׁנוּ בְּמִצְוֹתָיו וְצִוָּנוּ לְהַדְלִיק
נֵר שֶׁל שַׁבָּת.

Ba-ruch a-ta, A-do-nai E-lo-hei-nu, me-lech ha-o-lam, a-sher ki-de-sha-nu be-mits-vo-tav ve-tsi-va-nu le-had-lik neir shel Sha-bat.

We Praise You, Adonai our God, Ruler of the universe, who makes us holy with mitzvot, and commands us to light the Shabbat lights.

(On Weekdays and Shabbat:)

The First Cup:
White Wine — The Renewal of Trees

Now it is still winter time.
In many places snow is on the ground
so our first cup of wine is white.

Story: The Wagon Driver's Blessing

Rabbi Wolf Zitomirer was an innkeeper in a village. A Jewish wagon
driver entered and asked for a glass of wine. When he was about to drink
it without saying a blessing, the Rabbi stopped him and said, "Do you
realize all that God had to do so that the grapes would grow and people
could make wine?" The man then said the blessing, and the Rabbi
answered, "Amen!"

(Attributed to *Me-orot HaGedolim*)

First Cup of Wine (white)

Before we drink this cup of wine we thank God who made the world full
of good things to eat and drink.

(On Weekdays:)

בָּרוּךְ אַתָּה, יְיָ אֱלֹהֵינוּ, מֶלֶךְ הָעוֹלָם, בּוֹרֵא פְּרִי הַגָּפֶן.

Ba-ruch a-ta, A-do-nai E-lo-hei-nu, me-lech ha-olam, bo-rei pe-ri ha-ga-fen.

We praise You, Adonai our God, Ruler of the universe, who causes juicy
grapes to grow.

(Drink Wine)

(On Shabbat:)

בָּרוּךְ אַתָּה, יְיָ אֱלֹהֵינוּ, מֶלֶךְ הָעוֹלָם, בּוֹרֵא פְּרִי הַגָּפֶן.
בָּרוּךְ אַתָּה, יְיָ אֱלֹהֵינוּ, מֶלֶךְ הָעוֹלָם, אֲשֶׁר קִדְּשָׁנוּ בְּמִצְוֹתָיו וְרָצָה בָנוּ, וְשַׁבַּת
קָדְשׁוֹ בְּאַהֲבָה וּבְרָצוֹן הִנְחִילָנוּ, זִכָּרוֹן לְמַעֲשֵׂה בְרֵאשִׁית. כִּי הוּא יוֹם תְּחִלָּה
לְמִקְרָאֵי קֹדֶשׁ, זֵכֶר לִיצִיאַת מִצְרָיִם. כִּי־בָנוּ בָחַרְתָּ וְאוֹתָנוּ קִדַּשְׁתָּ מִכָּל־הָעַמִּים,
וְשַׁבַּת קָדְשְׁךָ בְּאַהֲבָה וּבְרָצוֹן הִנְחַלְתָּנוּ. בָּרוּךְ אַתָּה, יְיָ, מְקַדֵּשׁ הַשַּׁבָּת.

Ba-ruch a-ta, A-do-nai E-lo-hei-nu, me-lech ha-o-lam, bo-rei pe-ri ha-ga-fen. Ba-ruch a-ta, A-do-nai E-lo-hei-nu, me-lech ha-o-lam a-sher ki-de-sha-nu be-mits-vo-tav ve-ra-tsa va-nu, ve-Sha-bat kod-sho be-a-ha-va u-ve-ra-tson hin-chi-la-nu zi-ka-ron le-ma-a-sei ve-rei-shit. Ki hu yom te-chi-la, le-mik-ra-ei ko-desh zei-cher li-tsi-at Mits-ra-yim. Ki va-nu va-char-ta ve-o-ta-nu ki-dash-ta mi-kol ha-a-mim, ve-Sha-bat kod-she-cha be-a-ha-va u-ve-ra-tson hin-chal-ta-nu. Ba-ruch a-ta, A-do-nai, me-ka-deish ha-Sha-bat.

We praise You, Adonai our God, Ruler of the universe, who causes juicy grapes to grow.

We praise You, Adonai our God, ruler of the universe, who makes us holy with mitzvot and gives us the holy Shabbat so that we will remember that God made the world. It is the first of the holy days, a reminder of the going out from Egypt. You have chosen us and blessed us by giving us Shabbat. We praise You, O God, who makes Shabbat a holy day.

(Drink Wine)

THE LAND — HA-ARETS

We thank You, God, for rain and forests,
for land and stream,
for the lush trees of summer,
for the bright snow-covered branches of winter.

We thank you, too, for the Land of Israel, as we read: "For Adonai your God is bringing you into a good land, a land of wheat and barley, of vines, and figs, a land of olive trees and honey; a land where you may eat all that you need."

(Deuteronomy 8.6-8)

Story: The Trees Choose Israel

When the Holy One created trees and grass, they were invited to choose where they wanted to grow.

Most of them wanted to grow on great mountains, in lush quiet valleys. They wanted comfort and honor.

But the olive and the fig, the date and the wheat all wanted to grow in a small dry land. "Why do you want to grow there?" asked the Creator of the world. They answered, "We have heard that Your people, the people of Israel, will be given the Land of Israel. We want to grow there because we want to help the people of Israel to make the desert bloom, cover its fields with wheat and grow green trees in its mountains and valleys. Then the people will be able to find shelter in the shade of trees and eat their fruit."

Story: Each Generation Plants

"When you come into the land you shall plant..." (Leviticus 19.23) The Holy One said to Israel, "Even though you will find the land full of good things, don't say, 'We will sit and not plant.' Rather be careful to plant trees. Just as you found trees which others had planted when you entered the land, so you should plant for your children. No one should say, 'I am old. How many more years will I live? Why should I be troubled for the sake of others?' Just as he found trees, he should add more by planting even if he is old."

(Midrash Tanchuma, Kedoshim 8)

51

The trees made the land beautiful
and our people took good care of the land;
but, other people came and took the land.
Our people were forced to go to other places;
yet, we always hoped we could go back
to the Land of Israel.

The prophet Amos taught: I will bring My people back to Israel. They shall plant
grapes and drink their wine; they shall plant gardens and eat their fruits.
(Amos 9)

The great hope of our people has come true.
Once again Jews plant in Israel.
Pine trees now cover mountains.
Fruits and vegetables grow in the desert.

Israel is Renewed

Israel is like the sycamore tree. Even after it is
chopped down and its stump is covered with
sand for a long time, the sycamore will begin to
grow again. So too, the Jewish people which has
been attacked and hurt, grows again in our time.

The Second Cup:
Pink Wine — The Renewal of Israel

In the early spring, the earth gets warmer. Pink wine reminds us that pink flowers now grow in the Land of Israel.

בָּרוּךְ אַתָּה, יְיָ אֱלֹהֵינוּ, מֶלֶךְ הָעוֹלָם, בּוֹרֵא פְּרִי הַגָּפֶן.

Ba-ruch a-ta, A-do-nai E-lo-hei-nu, me-lech ha-o-lam, bo-rei pe-ri ha-ga-fen.
We praise You, Adonai our God, Ruler of the universe, who causes juicy grapes to grow.

(Drink Wine)

𝄞 Erets Zavat Chalav p. 77

אֶרֶץ זָבַת חָלָב
חָלָב וּדְבַשׁ

E-rets za-vat cha-lav
cha-lav u-de-vash. (4x)

אֶרֶץ זָבַת חָלָב
זָבַת חָלָב וּדְבַשׁ

E-rets za-vat cha-lav
za-vat cha-lav u-de-vash. (2x)
"...a land flowing with milk and honey."

(Deuteronomy 11.9)

TORAH — THE TREE OF LIFE

Trees live a long, long time. Some trees live for five hundred or even two thousand years.

The Torah is like a tree because it lives a very, very long time.

Trees give us shade to sit in and fruit to eat.

Torah helps us live a good life. It keeps our people alive.

Torah tells of the land of Israel, where our kings and queens and prophets lived; the land which Jews have rebuilt today.

That is why the Torah is called the Tree of Life.

𝄞 Eits Chayim p. 78

עֵץ־חַיִּים הִיא לַמַּחֲזִיקִים בָּהּ,
וְתֹמְכֶיהָ מְאֻשָּׁר.
דְּרָכֶיהָ דַרְכֵי־נֹעַם,
וְכָל־נְתִיבוֹתֶיהָ שָׁלוֹם.

Eits cha-yim hi la-ma-cha-zi-kim ba,
ve-to-me-che-ha me-u-shar.
De-ra-che-ha dar-chei no-am,
ve-chol ne-ti-vo-te-ha sha-lom.

It is a tree of life to those who grasp it,
and whoever holds on to it is happy.
Its ways are pleasant ways,
and all its paths, peaceful.

(Proverbs 3.17-18)

FRUIT OF GOD'S EARTH

We thank You, God, for the world You have made.

We thank You for the Land of Israel.

You made buds to form, beautiful flowers and ripe fruit to grow.

We thank You for the fruit we are about to eat.

Fruit With Shells

Nuts, Etrogs, Pomegranates, Oranges, Grapefruit

(Read the passage[s] for at least one fruit with shells.)

Almonds and Other Nuts

The First to Awaken

The almond tree is the first tree to greet Tu BiShevat. In Israel it is the first to awaken out of its winter sleep. By Tu BiShevat it is already full of flowers.

I said to the almond tree, "Sister, speak to me of God," and the almond tree blossomed.

(Attributed to N. Kazantazakis)

Hashekeidiya p. 79

הַשְׁקֵדִיָּה פּוֹרַחַת
וְשֶׁמֶשׁ פָּז זוֹרַחַת.
צִפֳּרִים מֵרֹאשׁ כָּל גַּג
מְבַשְּׂרוֹת אֶת בֹּא הֶחָג.
טוּ בִּשְׁבָט הִגִּיעַ חַג הָאִילָנוֹת

Ha-she-kei-di-ya po-ra-chat,
ve-she-mesh paz zo-ra-chat.
Tsi-po-rim mei-rosh kol gag,
me-va-se-rot et bo he-chag.
Tu Bi-Shevat hi-gi-a, chag ha-il-a-not. (2x)

The almond tree is blooming
'neath the golden sun.
Birds sing from every roof
telling us the time has come.
Tu BiShevat has come, the holiday of trees.

Israel and Walnuts

Rabbi Tarfon said that the people of Israel
are like a pile of walnuts. If one walnut is
removed, each and every walnut in the
pile will move.

*When a single Jew is in trouble, every
other Jew feels the trouble too.*
(Avot DeRabbi Natan 18.1)

Etrog

The etrog is very special. After the holiday of Sukkot was over, we put
cloves in it and saved it until now. It still smells good.

בָּרוּךְ אַתָּה, יְיָ אֱלֹהֵינוּ, מֶלֶךְ הָעוֹלָם, בּוֹרֵא מִינֵי בְשָׂמִים.

Ba-ruch a-ta, A-do-nai E-lo-hei-nu, me-lech ha-o-lam, bo-rei mi-nei ve-sa-mim.
We Praise You, Adonai our God, Ruler of the Universe, who causes all
spices to grow.

(Pass etrog and enjoy fragrance)

Blessing on Eating Fruit

The first kind of fruit we taste has a shell which cannot be eaten.
This shell protects the fruit inside, just as a young child is protected by
its parents.

בָּרוּךְ אַתָּה, יְיָ אֱלֹהֵינוּ, מֶלֶךְ הָעוֹלָם, בּוֹרֵא פְּרִי הָעֵץ.

Ba-ruch a-ta, A-do-nai E-lo-hei-nu, me-lech ha-o-lam, bo-rei pe-ri ha-eits.

We praise You, Adonai our God, Ruler of the universe, who causes trees to bear fruit.

בָּרוּךְ אַתָּה, יְיָ אֱלֹהֵינוּ, מֶלֶךְ הָעוֹלָם, שֶׁהֶחֱיָנוּ וְקִיְּמָנוּ וְהִגִּיעָנוּ לַזְּמַן הַזֶּה.

Ba-ruch a-ta, A-do-nai E-lo-hei-nu, me-lech ha-o-lam, she-he-che-ya-nu, ve-ki-ye-ma-nu ve-hi-gi-a-nu la-ze-man ha-zeh.

We praise You, Adonai our God, ruler of the universe, for giving us life, for sustaining us, and for enabling us to reach this season.

(Enjoy nuts and other fruit with shells.)

Fruit With Pits

Dates, Olives, Apricots, Peaches, Plums/Prunes

(Read the passage[s] for at least one fruit with pits.)

Date Palm

Israel Is Like a Date Palm

The date palm tree (*tamar*) is a very important tree, because every part of it can be used, every part is needed.

So it is with Israel: each community, each person, each child is important; every one is needed.

(*Numbers Rabba* 3.1)

𝄞 Tsadik Katamar p. 82

Tsa-dik ka-ta-mar yif-rach,
ke-e-rets ba-Le-va-non yis-geh.
She-tu-lim be-veit A-do-nai,
be-chats-rot E-lo-hei-nu yaf-ri-chu.
Od ye-nu-vun be-sei-va,
de-shei-nim ve-ra-a-na-nim yih-yu,
le-ha-gid ki ya-shar A-do-nai,
tsu-ri ve-lo av-la-ta bo.

צַדִּיק כַּתָּמָר יִפְרָח
כְּאֶרֶז בַּלְּבָנוֹן יִשְׂגֶּה:
שְׁתוּלִים בְּבֵית יְהֹוָה
בְּחַצְרוֹת אֱלֹהֵינוּ יַפְרִיחוּ:
עוֹד יְנוּבוּן בְּשֵׂיבָה
דְּשֵׁנִים וְרַעֲנַנִּים יִהְיוּ:
לְהַגִּיד כִּי־יָשָׁר יְהֹוָה
צוּרִי וְלֹא־עַוְלָתָה בּוֹ:

Those who are just and fair shall bloom like a date palm;
they shall grow like a cedar in Lebanon;
planted in the house of the Holy One,
they will be close to God.

(From Psalm 92)

Olive Tree

Hope for All

The olive tree was always a sign of hope. Long, long ago, there was a great flood. Water covered most of the world. Noah brought animals onto his ark to save them. When the rain stopped, Noah sent out a dove to see if there was any dry land. "The dove came back to him toward evening, and there in its bill was a leaf it had picked from an olive tree!"
(Genesis 8.11)

Then Noah and his family knew that they would soon be able to leave the ark.

(Choose from the following:)

𝄞 Atsei Zeitim p. 83

עֲצֵי זֵתִים עוֹמְדִים.

A-tsei zei-tim om-dim.

Olive trees are standing.

𝄞 Jerusalem of Gold p. 84

The olive trees that stand in silence
Upon the hills of time,
To hear the voices of the city
As bells of evening chime.
The shofar sounding from the temple
To call the world to prayer,
The shepherd pauses in the valley
And peace is everywhere.

Chorus

יְרוּשָׁלַיִם שֶׁל זָהָב
וְשֶׁל נְחֹשֶׁת וְשֶׁל אוֹר
הֲלֹא לְכָל שִׁירַיִךְ
אֲנִי כִּנּוֹר

Ye-ru-sha-la-yim shel za-hav
Veshel ne-cho-shet ve-shel or,
Ha-lo le-chol shi-ra-yich
A-ni ki-nor.

The water well for those who thirsted,
The ancient market square;
Your golden sun that lights the future
For all men everywhere.
How many songs, how many stories

The stony hills recall,
Around her heart my city carries
A lonely ancient wall.

Chorus

And far away beyond the desert
A thousand suns will glow;
We shall be going to the Jordan
By way of Jericho.
My simple voice cannot acclaim thee,
Too weak the words I choose.
Jerusalem, if I forget thee
May my right hand its cunning lose.

Chorus

(Naomi Shemer)

Blessing on Eating Fruit

The second kind of fruit we taste has a hard pit inside.

בָּרוּךְ אַתָּה, יְיָ אֱלֹהֵינוּ, מֶלֶךְ הָעוֹלָם, בּוֹרֵא פְּרִי הָעֵץ.

Ba-ruch a-ta, A-do-nai E-lo-hei-nu, me-lech ha-o-lam bo-rei pe-ri ha-eits.
We Praise You, Adonai our God, Ruler of the universe, who causes trees
to bear fruit.

(Enjoy fruit such as olives and dates.)

Entirely Edible Fruit

Figs, Raisins, Strawberries, Apples, Pears, Carob

Figs

Symbol of Peace

The Bible speaks of the fig tree in a time of peace. No one
will go off to war.

But all shall sit
under their grapevine or fig tree
with no one to disturb them.

(Micah 4.3-4)

(Choose from the following:)

♪ **Lo Yisa Goi** p. 86

לֹא יִשָּׂא גוֹי אֶל גּוֹי חֶרֶב,
לֹא יִלְמְדוּ עוֹד מִלְחָמָה.

Lo yi-sa goi el goi che-rev,
lo yil-me-du od mil-cha-ma.

Nation shall not take up
sword against nation;
they shall never again know war.

(Micah 4.3)

Veyashvu Ish p. 87

וְיָשְׁבוּ אִישׁ תַּחַת גַּפְנוֹ
וְתַחַת תְּאֵנָתוֹ
וְאֵין מַחֲרִיד

Ve-ya-she-vu ish ta-chat ga-fe-no
ve-ta-chat te-ei-na-to
ve-ein ma-cha-rid.

They shall sit, everyone under their
grapevine or fig tree with no one to disturb them.

(Micah 4.4)

Story: Plant for the Future

Once an old man was planting a fig tree when a Roman general happened to pass by. He laughed at the old man and said, "You Jews are stupid. Don't you realize it will take twenty years before that tree will grow enough to give fruit, and you will be long dead by then?"

The old man answered, "When I was a small child I could eat fruit because those who came before me planted trees. Shouldn't I do the same thing for the children who come after me?"

The general said, "If you live long enough to eat figs from this tree, let me know." In a few years the trees produced figs, and the old man lived long enough to enjoy them. He filled a basket and brought them to the general who honored him.

The general's servants were surprised that he would show honor to a Jew, but the

general told them, "His Creator honors him with long life and beautiful trees. I should honor him too."

(Leviticus Rabba 25.5)

Ki Tavo-u p. 88

וְכִי תָבוֹאוּ אֶל הָאָרֶץ,
וּנְטַעְתֶּם כָּל עֵץ תְּחִלָּה.
וְנָתַן הָעֵץ פִּרְיוֹ
וְהָאָרֶץ יְבוּלָה.
עֵת לִנְטוֹעַ אִילָנוֹת.

Ki ta-vo-u el ha-a-rets
u-ne-ta-a-tem kol eits te-chi-la.
Ve-na-tan ha-eits pir-yo
ve-ha-a-rets ye-vu-la.
Eit lin-to-a i-la-not. (2x)

When you come to the land
and plant trees,
each tree shall give its fruit
and the land shall give its abundance.
It is time to plant trees.

Blessing on Eating Fruit

We can eat all of the third kind of fruit we taste.

בָּרוּךְ אַתָּה, יְיָ אֱלֹהֵינוּ, מֶלֶךְ הָעוֹלָם, בּוֹרֵא פְּרִי הָעֵץ.

Ba-ruch a-ta, A-do-nai E-lo-hei-nu, me-lech ha-o-lam bo-rei pe-ri ha-eits.
We praise You, Adonai our God, Ruler of the universe, who causes trees to bear fruit.

(Enjoy fruit such as figs, raisins, apples, pears, carob.)

The Third Cup:
Light Red Wine — Israel's Spring Fruit

Red wine reminds us that in the Land of Israel, the first spring fruit is ripening. Strawberries, melons and apricots are picked; red flowers cover the ground like a blanket.

בָּרוּךְ אַתָּה, יְיָ אֱלֹהֵינוּ, מֶלֶךְ הָעוֹלָם, בּוֹרֵא פְּרִי הַגָּפֶן.

Ba-ruch a-ta, A-do-nai El-o-hei-nu, me-lech ha-o-lam, bo-rei pe-ri ha-ga-fen.

We praise You, Adonai our God, who causes juicy grapes to grow.

(Drink wine.)

🎼 **Havu Lanu Yayin** p. 89

הָבוּ לָנוּ יַיִן, יַיִן
לֹא שָׁתִינוּ עוֹד עֲדַיִן
הָבוּ לָנוּ יַיִן וְתִירוֹשׁ.

Ha-vu la-nu ya-yin, ya-yin,
lo sha-ti-nu od a-da-yin.
Ha-vu la-nu ya-yin ve-ti-rosh.

Give us wine,
for we have not sipped it yet.
Give us wine to drink.

A FESTIVE MEAL
Hamotzi

Wheat and barley,
rye and oats,
and all grains for bread,
grow in God's rich earth.

בָּרוּךְ אַתָּה, יְיָ אֱלֹהֵינוּ, מֶלֶךְ הָעוֹלָם, הַמּוֹצִיא לֶחֶם מִן הָאָרֶץ.

Ba-ruch a-ta, A-donai E-lo-hei-nu, me-lech ha-o-lam ha-mo-tsi le-chem min ha-a-rets.

We praise You, Adonai our God, Ruler of the world, who brings forth bread from the earth.

(Meal is Served)

63

THANKFULNESS

Thankfulness in Words

Praise for Field and Fruit

Praised are You, our God,
for the fruit of the vine,

For the fruits of trees,
for the vegetables from the field,

For the good land You have given
that we might eat of its fruit.
As it is written:

"And you shall eat your fill
And praise the name of Adonai, your God."

(Joel 2.26)

Fueled

(Sometimes we are so excited about the
things people have made, that we forget
what a wonderful world God has created.)

Fueled
by a million
man-made
wings of fire —
the rocket tore a tunnel
through the sky —
and everybody cheered.
Fueled

only by a thought from God —
the seedling
urged its way
through the thickness of black —
and as it pierced
the heavy ceiling of the soil —
up into outer space
no
one
even clapped.

(Marcy Hans)

Story: Which Blessing for a Tree?

A woman was traveling in the desert. She was hungry, tired and thirsty when she came to a tree whose fruits were sweet, its shade was pleasant and a stream of water flowed beneath it. She ate of its fruit, drank of the water, and rested under its shade. When she was about to continue her journey, she said, "Tree, with what shall I bless you? Shall I say,

'May your fruit be sweet?' It is sweet already. Shall I say, 'May a stream of water flow beneath you?' A stream of water already flows beneath you. Shall I say, 'May your shade be pleasant?' It is already pleasant. Therefore, I say, 'May all the trees which come from you be like you.'"
(Ta'anit 5b-6a)

Birkat Hamazon

רַבּוֹתַי, נְבָרֵךְ!

Ra-bo-tai ne-va-reich.

יְהִי שֵׁם יְיָ מְבֹרָךְ מֵעַתָּה וְעַד עוֹלָם.

Ye-hi sheim A-do-nai me-vo-rach mei-a-ta ve-ad o-lam.

בִּרְשׁוּת מָרָנָן וְרַבָּנָן וְרַבּוֹתַי, נְבָרֵךְ (אֱלֹהֵינוּ) שֶׁאָכַלְנוּ מִשֶּׁלּוֹ.

Bi-re-shut ma-ra-nan ve-ra-ba-nan ve-ra-bo-tai, ne-va-reich E-lo-hei-nu she-a-chal-nu mi-she-lo.

בָּרוּךְ (אֱלֹהֵינוּ) שֶׁאָכַלְנוּ מִשֶּׁלּוֹ וּבְטוּבוֹ חָיִינוּ.

Ba-ruch E-lo-hei-nu she-a-chal-nu mi-she-lo u-ve-tu-vo cha-yi-nu.

Let us praise God.

May God's name be praised now and forever.

Praised is our God who has given us food to eat.

Praised is our God who has given us many wonderful gifts.

בָּרוּךְ אַתָּה, יְיָ, אֱלֹהֵינוּ מֶלֶךְ הָעוֹלָם, הַזָּן אֶת הָעוֹלָם כֻּלּוֹ בְּטוּבוֹ; בְּחֵן בְּחֶסֶד וּבְרַחֲמִים, הוּא נוֹתֵן לֶחֶם לְכָל בָּשָׂר, כִּי לְעוֹלָם חַסְדּוֹ. וּבְטוּבוֹ הַגָּדוֹל תָּמִיד לֹא חָסַר לָנוּ, וְאַל יֶחְסַר לָנוּ מָזוֹן לְעוֹלָם וָעֶד בַּעֲבוּר שְׁמוֹ הַגָּדוֹל; כִּי הוּא אֵל זָן וּמְפַרְנֵס לַכֹּל, וּמֵטִיב לַכֹּל, וּמֵכִין מָזוֹן לְכָל בְּרִיּוֹתָיו אֲשֶׁר בָּרָא. בָּרוּךְ אַתָּה, יְיָ, הַזָּן אֶת הַכֹּל.

Ba-ruch a-ta, A-do-nai E-lo-hei-nu, me-lech ha-o-lam, ha-zan et ha-o-lam ku-lo be-tu-vo be-chein, be-che-sed, u-ve-ra-cha-mim. Hu no-tein le-chem le-chol ba-sar, ki le-o-lam chas-do. U-ve-tu-vo ha-ga-dol ta-mid lo cha-sar la-nu, ve-al ye-che-sar la-nu ma-zon le-o-lam va-ed, ba-a-vur she-mo ha-ga-dol. Ki hu Eil zan u-me-far-neis la-kol u-mei-tiv la-kol u-mei-chin ma-zon le-chol be-ri-yo-tav a-sher ba-ra. Ba-ruch a-ta, A-do-nai, ha-zan et ha-kol.

Praised is Adonai, our God, Ruler of the world who gives food to all.

Praised is the Source of all food.

"When you have eaten and are satisfied, then bless Adonai your God, who has given you this good land."

Praised is Adonai, our God, for the land and for the food.

Our God and God of all ages, remember Your people Israel on this day of Tu BiShevat. May it be a time of love and goodness, life and peace.

This day remember us for well-being.
This day bless us with Your nearness.
This day help us to a fuller life.

Let us all say, "Amen."

66

וּבְנֵה יְרוּשָׁלַיִם עִיר הַקֹדֶשׁ בִּמְהֵרָה בְיָמֵינוּ. בָּרוּךְ אַתָּה, יְיָ, בּוֹנֵה בְרַחֲמָיו יְרוּשָׁלָיִם. אָמֵן.

U-ve-nei Ye-ru-sha-la-yim ir ha-ko-desh bi-me-hei-ra be-ya-mei-nu. Ba-ruch a-ta, A-do-nai, bo-neh be-ra-cha-mav Ye-ru-sha-la-yim. A-men.

O let Jerusalem, the holy city, be renewed in our time. Praised is Adonai, by whose compassion we will see Jerusalem renewed and at peace. Amen.

(On Shabbat)

הָרַחֲמָן, הוּא יַנְחִילֵנוּ יוֹם שֶׁכֻּלוֹ שַׁבָּת וּמְנוּחָה לְחַיֵּי הָעוֹלָמִים:

Ha-ra-cha-man, hu yan-chi-lei-nu yom she-ku-lo sha-bat u-me-nu-cha le-cha-yei ha-o-la-mim.

May God always bless us with Shabbaths of rest and peace.

May God bless all of us who have eaten at this table.

עוֹשֶׂה שָׁלוֹם בִּמְרוֹמָיו, הוּא יַעֲשֶׂה שָׁלוֹם עָלֵינוּ וְעַל כָּל יִשְׂרָאֵל. וְאִמְרוּ: אָמֵן.

O-seh sha-lom bi-me-ro-mav, hu ya-a-seh sha-lom a-lei-nu ve-al kol Yis-ra-eil, ve-im-ru: A-men.

May God bring peace to us, and all the world.

The Fourth Cup:
Dark Red Wine — The Cup of Thankfulness

In summer the flowers are in full bloom, field and tree give their fruit. We drink this darkest-red cup of wine with thanks for the richness of God's land.

בָּרוּךְ אַתָּה, יְיָ אֱלֹהֵינוּ, מֶלֶךְ הָעוֹלָם, בּוֹרֵא פְּרִי הַגָּפֶן.

Ba-ruch a-ta, A-do-nai E-lo-hei-nu, me-lech ha-o-lam, bo-rei pe-ri ha-ga-fen.

Praised are You, Adonai our God, ruler of the universe who causes juicy grapes to grow.

(Drink Wine)

Thankfulness in Deeds

Tithes

Keren Peirot — Food Fund

With new buds formed and new rains falling, Tu BiShevat was the new year for fruit. It was the beginning of the year for bringing fruit to the Temple in Jerusalem, and for giving food to the poor.

The Torah reminds us to give some of what we have to others who are hungry.

We may "eat choice foods and drink sweet drinks," but we should "send portions to those who have nothing."

(Nehemiah 8.10)

(Food for the hungry may be provided in several ways: an add-on "tithe" of the cost of the food for the Seder, bringing nourishing non-perishable food items for a local food pantry, an appeal for voluntary contributions, etc.)

Planting

Imitate God

From the very beginning of the creation of the world, God was busy planting, so when you enter the land you too shall plant.

(*Leviticus Rabba* 25.3)

Plant for Passover

(Parsley or romaine, which will be used on Passover, can be planted. Prepare a small cup of soil for each family. Parsley or romaine seeds should be provided for planting.)

O God, we thank You for earth and seed; for all things that grow. We thank You that we are Your partners in planting.

We praise You, Adonai our God, for small seeds and rich earth.

(Plant seeds)

♩ The Planting Song p. 90

There are trees and plants that give us
nearly everything we need,
but don't forget they started out
as tiny little seeds.
You can throw them in the air
or you can hold them in your hand,
but someday those tiny seeds will grow
and trees will fill the land.

Chorus

So take a little seed,
plant it in the ground,
(and that seed will grow as the seasons flow,
with branches all around.) (2x)

It is written in the Torah,
when we saw the promised land,
we planted trees at every turn,
for this was God's command.

And today in modern Israel,
where they made the desert bloom,
in such a tiny country,
for a tree there's always room.

Chorus

In the Talmud is a saying
written many years ago,
that every plant has a special star
to teach it how to grow.
If you happen to be planting
and someone comes along,
finish what you're doing
and together sing this song.

(Jeffrey Klepper)

Plant Trees in Israel

Our God and God of our fathers and mothers, we are thankful for the renewal of the land of our ancestors. We are thankful that we can help plant forests and make the land blossom.

May You bless the land and all its trees with beauty, plenty and peace.

(It is customary to celebrate Tu Bishevat by planting trees in Israel through the Jewish National Fund, the agency responsible for afforestation and land reclamation in Israel. To purchase trees, tree-planting forms can be obtained through your local Jewish National Fund Office.)

Planting and Hope.

There is a custom that at the birth of a girl, a cypress tree is planted and at the birth of a boy, a cedar tree is planted. When a couple is married, they stand under a chupa made of wood from the trees planted at their birth.

It's Time For Planting p. 91

Boys and girls, it's time for planting.
Each one take a baby tree.
In the warm earth place it gently.
La, la, la, la, la, la, la, la,
Tu Bishevat, Tu Bishevat!
La, la, la, la, la, la, la, la,
Tu Bishevat, Tu Bishevat!

Turn Turn Turn p. 92

Chorus

To everything, turn, turn, turn
There is a season, turn, turn, turn
And a time to every purpose under heaven

A time to be born, a time to die
A time to plant, a time to reap
A time to kill, a time to heal
A time to laugh, a time to weep

Chorus

A time to build up, a time to break down
A time to dance, a time to mourn
A time to cast away stones
A time to gather stones together

Chorus

A time to love, a time to hate
A time of war, a time of peace
A time you may embrace
A time to refrain from embracing

Chorus

A time to gain, a time to lose
A time to rend, a time to sew
A time for love, a time for hate
A time for peace
I swear it's not too late

Chorus

(Pete Seeger, based on Ecclesiastes 3.1-8)

The Messiah

Planting is so important. If you were about to plant a tree, and you were told that the Messiah had come, first plant the tree, then go out to greet the Messiah.

Etein Bamidbar p. 94

אֶתֵּן בַּמִדְבָּר נֶטַע אֶרֶז,
שִׁטָּה וַהֲדַס וְעֵץ שָׁמֶן,
אָשִׂים בַּעֲרָבָה בְּרוֹשׁ
תִּדְהָר וּתְאַשּׁוּר יַחְדָּיו.

E-tein ba-mid-bar ne-ta e-rez e-rez
shita ve-ha-das ve-eits sha-men sha-men
A-sim ba-a-ra-va be-rosh (2x)
E-ten ba-mid-bar ne-ta e-rez e-rez
shi-ta ve-ha-das ve-eits sha-men sha men.
A-sim ba-a-ra va be-rosh,
be-rosh tid-har u-te-a-shur yach-dav.

I will put a cedar plant in the desert, acacia and myrtle and an oil-producing tree.
I will put a fir tree in the wilderness, elm and cypress together.

Custodians of God's World

Story: Do Not Destroy

When God led Adam through the Garden of Eden, God told him, "I made My beautiful and glorious world for your sake. Take care not to hurt or destroy My world, for if you do, there is no one to fix it after you."

(Ecclesiastes Rabba 7

♪ Eili, Eili p. 76

אֵלִי, אֵלִי,

שֶׁלֹּא יִגָּמֵר לְעוֹלָם

הַחוֹל וְהַיָּם,

רִשְׁרוּשׁ שֶׁל הַמַּיִם,

בְּרַק הַשָּׁמַיִם,

תְּפִלַּת הָאָדָם.

Ei-li, Ei-li,
she-lo yi-ga-meir le-ol-am
ha-chol ve-ha-yam,
rish-rush shel ha-ma-yim,
be-rak ha-sha-ma-yim,
te-fi-lat ha-a-dam. (2x)

O God, our God,
I pray that these things never end:
The sand and the sea,
The rush of the waters,
The crash of the heavens,
The prayers of the heart. (2x)

The Tree Song
Try to be more like a tree,
it knows just when to bend.
and it knows when you should take a stand,
helping a stranger, helping a friend.

Giving shelter to those in need by standing
straight and tall, reach out a hand and help
someone before they take a fall.

(Joan Besser)

Prayer for Your World

May it be Your will, Adonai our God and God of our fathers and mothers, that all fruit trees be filled with beautiful buds and blossoms.

May they be renewed each year to grow and give the fruit of goodness and sweetness.

May we all take good care of Your world.

May we enjoy and share the fruit of Your earth.

𝄞 Hatikva p. 95

כָּל עוֹד בַּלֵּבָב פְּנִימָה
נֶפֶשׁ יְהוּדִי הוֹמִיָּה,
וּלְפַאֲתֵי מִזְרָח קָדִימָה
עַיִן לְצִיּוֹן צוֹפִיָּה.
עוֹד לֹא אָבְדָה תִּקְוָתֵנוּ,
הַתִּקְוָה שְׁנוֹת אַלְפַּיִם,
לִהְיוֹת עַם חָפְשִׁי בְּאַרְצֵנוּ,
אֶרֶץ צִיּוֹן וִירוּשָׁלַיִם.

So long as still within the inmost heart
a Jewish spirit sings,
so long as the eye looks eastward
toward Zion,
our hope is not lost —
that hope of two thousand years,
to be a free people in our land,
the land of Zion and Jerusalem

Kol od ba-lei-vav pe-ni-ma
ne-fesh Ye-hu-di ho-mi-ya,
u-le-fa-a-tei miz-rach ka-di-ma
a-yin le-Tsi-yon tso-fi-ya,
od lo av-da tik-va-tei-nu,
ha-tik-va she-not al-pa-yim
(lih-yot am chof-shi be-art-sei-nu
e-rets Tsi-yon vi-Ye-ru-sha-la-yim.) 2x

TU BISHEVAT SONGS

Hinei Ma Tov

arr. C. Davidson

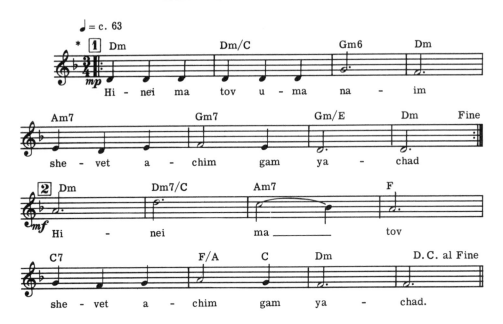

Hi - nei ma tov u - ma na - im

she - vet a - chim gam ya - chad

Hi - nei ma _____ tov

she - vet a - chim gam ya - chad.

* May be sung as a round.

74

Nitzanim Niru

Music: Nachum Heiman

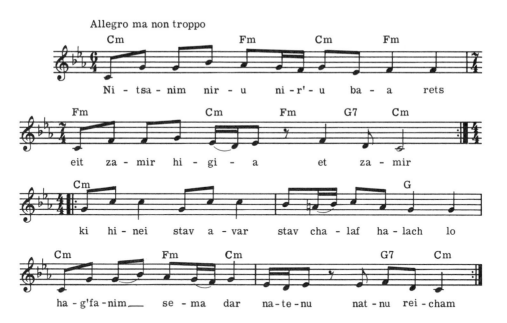

Allegro ma non troppo

Ni – tsa – nim nir – u ni – r' – u ba – a rets

eit za – mir hi – gi – a et za – mir

ki hi – nei stav a – var stav cha – laf ha – lach lo

ha – g'fa – nim___ se – ma dar na – te – nu nat – nu rei – cham

Eili, Eili

Expressively (♩ = c. 92)

Ei - li, Ei - li she - lo yi - ga - meir le - o -
O God, my God, I pray that these things nev - er

lam ha - chol ve - ha - yam rish - rush shel ha -
end: The sand and the sea, the__ rush of the__

ma - yim, be - rak ha - sha - ma - yim te - fi - lat ha - a -
wa - ters, the__ crash of the__ heav - ens, the__ prayer of the

dam; ha - chol ve - ha - yam rish - rush shel ha - ma - yim, be -
heart. The sand and the sea, the__ rush of the wa - ters, the

rak ha - sha - ma - yim te - fi - lat ha - a - dam.
crash of the heav - ens, the prayer of the heart.

Lyrics: Traditional

Erets Zavat Chalav

Music: Eliahu Gamliel

Eits Chayim

arr. C. Davidson

Eits cha - yim _____ hi la - ma - cha — zi - kim, ba ve -
chei — ha dar' - chei _____ no - am ve -

to — me - che ha me - u — shar. De - ra -
chol ne - ti - vo - te ha _____ sha - lom

Ha - shi - vei - nu _____ A - do - nai ei — le - cha ve -

na - shu - va, cha - deish, cha - deish _____ ya - mei - nu, cha -

deish _____ ya - mei - nu ke - ke - dem.

Lyrics: Israel Dushman

Hashekeidiya

Music: Menashe Ravina

Allegro moderato

D

Hash - kei - di - ya po - ra - chat ve - she-mesh paz zo - ra - chat
The al-mond tree is bloom - ing___ 'neath the gold-en sun ___

Bm | **D** | **A7** | **D**

tsi - po - rim me - rosh kol gag   me - vas-rot et bo he - chag
Birds___ sing from ev -'ry roof   tell - ing us the time has come

Bm **G** **D** **Bm** **A**

Tu bi - shevat hi - gi - a   chag ha - i - la - not
Tu bi - shevat has come the   hol - i - day of trees

Bm **G** **D** **A7** **D**

Tu bi - shevat hi - gi - a   chag ha - i - la - not.
Tu bi - shevat has come the   hol - i - day of trees.

Lyrics: Traditional

El Ginat Egōz

Music: Sara Levy-Tanai

El gi-nat e - gōz ya - ra - de - ti _____ lir' -

ōt be - i - bei ha - na - - chal lir' - ōt ha - fa - re - cha ha -

ge - fen hei - nei - tsu ha - ri - mō - nim

Y. Orland

Eits Rimon

Adapted from a Persian melody by Y. Admon. Copyright© 1972 by Mifalei Tarbut ve Chinuch.

Tsadik Katamar

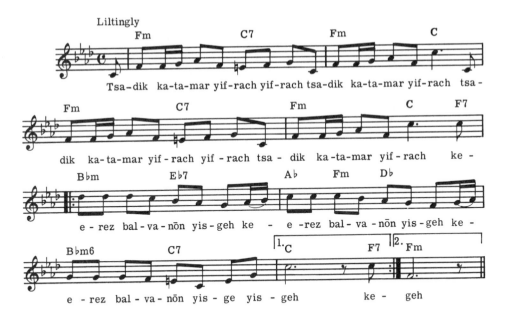

Tsa-dik ka-ta-mar yif-rach yif-rach tsa-dik ka-ta-mar yif-rach tsa-

dik ka-ta-mar yif-rach yif-rach tsa-dik ka-ta-mar yif-rach ke-

e-rez bal-va-nōn yis-geh ke — e-rez bal-va-nōn yis-geh ke-

e-rez bal-va-nōn yis-ge yis-geh ke-geh

Traditional

Atsei Zeitim

A-tsei zei-tim om-dim A-tsei zei-tim om-dim A-tsei zei-tim om-dim

Ah! Ah! _____

A-tsei zei-tim om-dim A-tsei zei-tim om-dim A-tsei zei-tim om-dim

Ah! _____ Ah! _____ Ah! Ah!

A-tsei zei-tim om-dim A-tsei zei-tim om-dim A-tsei zei-tim om-dim

La, la, la, la, la,_ la, la, A-tsei zei-tim om-dim la, la, la, la, la,_ la, la,

A-tsei zei-tim om-dim A-tsei zei-tim om-dim A-tsei zei-tim om-dim

A-tsei zei-tim om-dim.

A-tsei zei-tim om-dim A-tsei zei-tim om-dim A-tsei zei-tim om-dim.

Jerusalem of Gold

Naomi Shemer

A - vir ha - rim tsa - lul ka - ya - yin ve - rei - ach o - ra -
The ol - ive trees that stand in si - lence up - on the hills of___
The wa - ter well for those who thirst - ed, the an - cient mar - ket___
And far a - way be - yond the des - ert a thou - sand suns will___

nim ni - sa be - ru - ach ha - ar - ba - yim im kol pa -
time, To hear the voic - es of the cit - y as bells of
square; Your gold - en sun that lights the fu - ture for all those
glow; We shall be go - ing to the Jor - dan by way of

a - mo - nim uv' - tar - dei - mat i - lan va - e - ven sh'vu -
eve - ning chime. The sho - far sound - ing from the tem - ple to
eve - ry - where; How man - y songs, how man - y sto - ries the
Jer - i - co. My sim - ple voice can - not ac - claim thee, too

ya ba - cha - lo - ma ha - ir a - sher ba - dad yo -
call the world to___ prayer, The shep - herd paus - es in the
ston - y hills re - call, A - round her heart my cit - y
weak the words I___ choose; Je - ru - sa - lem if I for -

she - vet u - ve - li - ba cho - ma Ye - ru - sha -
val - ley and peace is eve - ry - where.
car - ries a lone - ly an - cient wall.
get thee may my right hand its cun - ning lose.

la - yim shel za - hav   ve - shel ne - cho - shet   ve - shel

or   ha - lo   le - chol   shi - ra - yich   a - ni   ki -

nor   Ye - ru   sha - nor   ra - yich   a -

ni ____ ki - nor _____   ki - nor

Lo Yisa Goi

Shalom Altman

Arr. C. Davidson

Resolutely

Lo yi-sa goi el goi che - rev, _____ lo yil-me-du od mil-cha-ma, _____ Lo yi-sa ma.
And ev-'ry man 'neath his vine and fig tree shall live in peace and un-a-fraid,_____ And ev-'ry fraid.

Lo yi-sa goi el goi che - rev, lo yil-me-du od _
And in-to plough-shares beat their swords. Na - tions_ shall make_

mil - cha - ma, lo yi - sa goi el goi che - rev
war no more, and in - to plough-shares beat their swords,

lo yil - me - du od_____ mil - cha - ma.
Na - tions shall make_ war no more.

D.C. al Fine

86

Veyashvu Ish

Ve - yash - vu ish ta - chat gaf - no____ ve - ta - chat te - ci - na - to____ ve - yash - vu ish ta - chat gaf - no____ ve - ta - chat te - ci - na - to____ Ah! ve - ein macha - rid____ Ah! ve - ein macha - rid.____

Daniel Freelander, Jeffrey Klepper

Ki Tavo-u

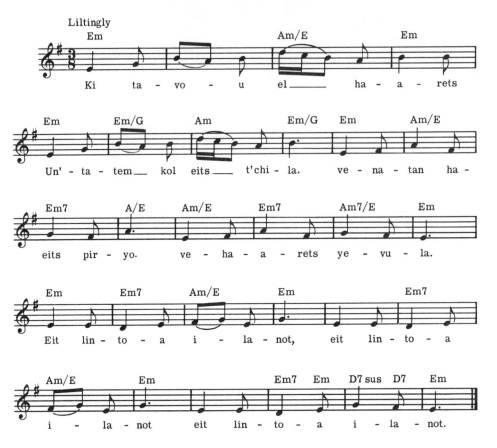

88

Matatyahu Shelem

Havu Lanu Yayin

M. Shelem

Joyously
Em

Ha - vu la - nu ya - yin ya - yin lo sha - ti - nu
Be - cha - yei - nu lo na - ku - ta af nich - ye ve -

Em   G   D   Em

od a - da - yin ha - vu la - nu ya - yin ve - ti - rosh____
lo na - mu - ta ma to - vim ya - fim cha - yei e - nosh____

Am   Em   C

U - ra u - ra tse ba - chur b'ma - chol nil - hav sis us -
Su - ra su - ra kol mar ne - fesh mar lei - vav su - ra

1. D   Am   2. D   Em

mach ba chur____ su - ra sur____

Copyright© Mifalei Tarbut Vechinuch, Israel

89

The Planting Song

Jeffrey Klepper

It's Time For Planting

B. Omer (Hatuli)

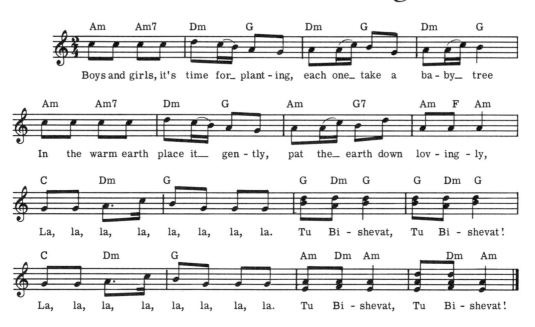

Boys and girls, it's time for_ plant - ing, each one_ take a ba - by_ tree

In the warm earth place it_ gen - tly, pat the_ earth down lov - ing - ly,

La, la, la, la, la, la, la, la. Tu Bi - shevat, Tu Bi - shevat!

La, la, la, la, la, la, la, la. Tu Bi - shevat, Tu Bi - shevat!

Turn, Turn, Turn

Pete Seeger

dance, a time to mourn; a time to cast a-way stones; a time to gath-er stones to-geth-er. To ev-'ry-

Verse 3

A time of love, a time of hate; a time of war, a time of peace; a time you may em-brace, a time to re-frain from em-brac-ing. To ev-'ry-

Verse 4

A time to gain, a time to lose; a time to rend, a time to sew; a time to love, a time to hate; a time for peace. I swear it's not too late. To ev-'ry-

Etein Bamidbar

E - tein ba-mid-bar ne-ta e-rez shi-ta ve-ha-das ve-eits sha-men a-sim be-a-ra-va be-rosh, a-sim be-a ra-va be-rosh.

E - tein ba-mid-bar ne-ta e-rez (e-rez) shi-ta ve-ha-das ve-eits sha-men a-sim be-a-ra-va (sha-men)

be-rosh, be-rosh tid-har-u, te-a-shur yach-dav.

Hatikva

Text: Chaim Stern

This Is Very Good

Jeffrey Klepper

When God made the world, and made it full of light; the sun to shine by day, the moon and stars by night. God made it full of life: li-lies, oaks, and trout, ti-gers and bears, spar-rows, hawks, ____ and apes. And God took clay from earth's four cor-ners to give it the breath of life ____ and God said: ____

Slightly faster

Tu Bishevat

Words and music:
Steven Carr Reuben

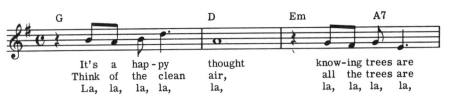

It's a hap - py thought, knowing trees are
Think of the clean air, all the trees are
La, la, la, la, la, la, la, la, la,

grow - ing._____ When it's Tu Bi - shevat
mak - ing._____ Tu Bi - shevat is here,
la, la._____ La, la, la, la, la,

na - ture's praise we're show - ing._____
Time for cel - e - bra ting._____
la, la, la, la, la, la._____